Wilfred Pickles

Invites You To
Have Another Go

Wilfred Pickles

Invites You To
Have Another Go

DAVID & CHARLES
Newton Abbot London North Pomfret (Vt) Vancouver

British Library Cataloguing in Publication Data

Pickles, Wilfred
  Wilfred Pickles invites you to have another go.
  1. Pickles, Wilfred   2. Broadcasters—Great
Britain—Biography
791.44′028′0924   HE8699.G7

  ISBN 0-7153-7393-5

Library of Congress Catalog Card Number:
77–85039

© Wilfred Pickles 1978

Printed in Great Britain
by Latimer Trend & Company Ltd Plymouth
for David & Charles (Publishers) Limited
Brunel House Newton Abbot Devon

Published in the United States of America
by David & Charles Inc
North Pomfret Vermont 05053 USA

Published in Canada
by Douglas David & Charles Limited
1875 Welch Street North Vancouver BC

CONTENTS

I was born on the cold grey hills in the days when life was
    stern,
When work had left the old hand loom and wages were hard
    to earn.
The lean days gripped my father's hearth with nothing to
    spend on books,
And the little I know was learned from folk in the ingle-nooks.
Too true that I have dimmed the light, too true that I have
    blurred the fair,
But maybe I have freshened the scene with a breath of
    moorland air.
But whatever is writ is writ, whether it be blessed or cursed,
Oh remember the little that is good, and forgive and forget the
    worst.

An Apology, Ammon Wrigley

FOREWORD

by The Rt Hon Lord Robens of Woldingham

There are few people who have the respect and affection of literally millions of people throughout the world, but Wilfred Pickles is one of them. The odd thing is that the vast majority of the millions have never clapped eyes upon him.

But they know him intimately. They know that he is a very kindly man who really believes that people matter. They know, too, that he is a man with a great sense of humour, that his amiability is sincere, and that his face is always creased in a smile. They know that he loves children and is concerned about the youngsters who are underprivileged and deprived. They know, too, that he is equally at home with people great and small.

How does it come about that they know all this if they have never met him or seen him on the television screen. The answer is—by the magic and the richness of his voice. The warmth of the broad vowels of northern folk, punctuated by the special distinctive Yorkshire habit of pronouncing a 'd' as a 't', and there you have it.

He reached the top of his adopted profession as actor and entertainer by dint of hard work and perseverance; his university was the experience of life, his triumphs he accepted with due modesty, his disappointments he bore with a smile He shared all the ups and downs with his much loved partner and stage collaborator, Mabel, to whom he has been married for nearly half a century.

9

What a privilege it has been for those of us who have known him and sat at table with them both.

A man who played many parts, from young man to grand-dad, in which Wilfred Pickles disappeared, and the character the playwright created emerged true to life—to the dialect reciter, who could bring his listener to laughter or to tears—all this and more besides with the impeccable perfection of a superb artist.

Off stage, Wilfred was not only an agreeable companion, but because he was well read and much experienced, a wonderful conversationalist. He had strong views about the importance of high standards and the importance of quality of manners and bearing in human behaviour; he hated injustice with a passion so sincere that one could feel the vibrations. Indeed, if he had turned to politics rather than to the stage, he would have reached the top rung of the ladder, as he did in the world of entertainment.

Through his art, he enriched the lives of countless thou-sands; he brought comfort to the thousands of lonely listeners, rich and poor alike, who listened and enjoyed his offerings on radio, television and the boards—this was the universal audience, young and old alike, who listened and applauded. The young grow up and continue to applaud with their children joining in. There never seems to have been a time when Wilfred was not around.

His contribution to the quality of life is immeasurable.

He's a Yorkshireman, and I'm a Lancastrian—in my language Wilfred Pickles is 'a gradely mon'—you'll enjoy reading him.

November, 1977

1 MAKE YOURSELF AT HOME

'Ladies and Gentlemen of Bingley, 'ow do, 'ow are yer?'
With these words I introduced the very first *Have a Go* programme in 1946. Little did anyone think then that they would
become part of radio history. Only the name of the place was
to alter, week by week, for twenty-one years in a show which
was originally intended to run for just six weeks. Today, over
ten years since the programme went off the air, and despite
such current catchphrases as 'Didn't he do well?' and 'Are
you being served?' I'm still stopped in the street to be asked
'Are yer coortin?' or someone will shout after me 'Give 'im
the money'.

And I'm still questioned about the show's astonishing
popularity, an appeal which went right across the board,
from children to pensioners, palaces—literally—to cottages,
board room to shop floor. To me it is clear that, unlike many
modern ultra-sophisticated quiz shows, relying on expensive
prizes and professional expertise, *Have a Go* was like the
American constitution, 'by the people, for the people and,
above all, of the people'. Simplicity was the keynote. Audience participation was paramount. Take, for instance, an
average programme like the one from Blackburn when the
formula was already an established success.

By this time we ranged all over the country looking for
suitable venues. Although the first broadcasts had come from
the north—Huddersfield, Sheffield, Chesterfield, Wallasey

and a dozen more towns and villages followed Bingley—very soon each BBC region was allotted a number of programmes, so that we covered Ireland, Scotland, Wales, the Midlands and the South in our efforts to be fair to everyone. Whilst prepared to go anywhere, and the less I knew about a place the better, I was not personally involved in the choice of location which was left to the producer in consultation with the head of Light Programmes. A local notable, say the youth leader or town clerk, was invited to be our on-the-spot organiser, to suggest a suitable meeting-place for the broadcast, to 'advertise' the show and distribute tickets. At the height of our success, of course, tickets were highly prized as often only a small number of the community could be accommodated in the village hall or local pub. I well remember the remark of one old woman queuing for her seat, in a bitter blizzard outside the Oldham Co-op. 'Well,' she remarked with some satisfaction, 'if we don't get a ticket, we might get pneumonia!'

Our local helper would get together about a dozen people who were interested in 'Having a Go' and these were invited to a teaparty on the Monday evening prior to the next day's show. Only half of this number would be needed for the actual broadcast, so we used this informal, chatty party as a means of deciding on the most suitable 'contestants'. We certainly were not looking for life-of-the-party types. It did not take me long to realise that the 'personalities' who were so sure of their repertoire, or the oddities with an axe to grind, were the ones who drifted to the side entrances, determined to catch the eye and edge their way into *Have a Go*. These were the very people we did not want.

There were impressive exceptions, however, the most striking perhaps being one determined old man who insisted in taking part in the programme from King George's Hall, Blackburn. The audience were already relaxed after our usual short concert which always prefaced the show, off-air,

to put people in the right mood. Our volunteers were waiting
to be conducted to the platform, when in hustled Ben Ainsworth, a real Lancastrian, as forthright as he was upright.
'Sithee', he called, coming straight up to me 'ah want to,
be in this 'ere quiz an' ah want to answer questions on tunes.
Ah only know eleven so ah've written 'em darn an' tha mon
pick four out o' that lot'! I chuckled as he handed me a page
torn from an old notebook. Ben would obviously be good
value at the microphone, so I copied down four of his tunes
and arranged to have them played.

Then, after the customary advice to the audience to clap
only when something was worth applauding—unlike the
floor managers on today's TV shows who actively encourage
applause—our producer gave the signal for the broadcast to
begin with the words 'And here he is, Wilfred Pickles'. Violet
Carson, now known to millions as the irrascible Ena Sharples
of *Coronation Street*, played the first notes of our familiar
signature tune, 'Have a Go, Joe, Come on and Have a Go' as
I led the audience in a general singsong before uttering the
words 'Ladies and Gentlemen of Blackburn, 'ow do, 'ow are
yer?'

Unable to contain his excitement, when his turn came Ben
Ainsworth fairly skipped onto the stage despite his grey hairs.
He told me he was seventy-three, and when I asked if he
were married he spoke up strongly: 'Ay, three times. She's
t'latest down theer. Her wi' t'white 'at. And she's a good
'un!, Three thousand voices roared.

What great appeal there was, and is, in the ungrudging
sincerity and unpretentiousness of such men and women who
never made the headlines. As ever, such frank and friendly
participation backed up my judgement that we were right
not to produce the programme in a studio. The people were
on their own doorstep so that the programme became a
family affair. Local people were up there giving Wilfred
Pickles as much as he gave them—and often more—so that

the applause that greeted most remarks was an expression of congratulation to a member of the family in his or her moment of achievement, and of admiration for the courage shown in facing up to questions at the microphone.

And it was Ben Ainsworth who provided the biggest laugh ever heard in *Have a Go*, or possibly in any programme since. In reply to the question 'What's your favourite drink?' with a great grin and shining eyes he retorted 'Tea wi' senna pods in'. And, as he stepped away, duly pocketing his winnings, he whispered, 'I weren't kiddin'. I sup it every mornin'.'

The ease with which Ben won his money is indicative of the general level of the quiz element of the programme. The questions were simple and up to date. We did not pretend to offer an alternative to *The Brains Trust*. Nor did we give fabulous prizes, the reward for success being a guinea, and the well-known phrase 'Give 'im the money, Mabel' representing more some small recognition of the performer's character than his correct answers to our pretty basic questions.

The finale of each programme came with the jackpot question, open to all who had taken part. Any money left over was automatically available, along with such local produce as scones, a traditional cake or a homemade garment, provided by the people of the district. By this time in the half-hour show I was keeping an eye firmly on the clock, as we went out live and to overrun was fatal. Fortunately we had the timing down to a fine art so that, as the applause for the jackpot winner died away, with just a minute or so to go, I stepped up to the microphone to say: 'And so we come to the end of this week's *Have a Go* which came to you from Blackburn, with Violet Carson at the piano, and this is your old pal Wilfred Pickles wishing you all good luck and good neet.' Then, as we all joined in with a chorus of 'Come round any old time and make yourself at home', the voices faded out and the Light Programme returned to scripted comedy.

I remain intensely proud of the success of *Have a Go*. It carried none of the imaginative fictions of the scriptwriter, just as there was none of the ordered tidiness that characterised so much of BBC output then and now. I appreciated that it would mean nothing to the listeners if someone told me that his uncle was the prime minister. But if this same man said, 'Our cat had kittens in my bowler hat this morning,' millions would appreciate the situation, one which could have happened to them.

It was the instinctive simplicity and homeliness of the everyday men and women interviewed that gave the programme its strength and vitality. While the lion's share of the credit for *Have a Go*'s success must go to these same ordinary people, I'm sure that my ability to bring out the best in them sprang from the fact that my own background was similar to theirs. All my life I have been fascinated by working people, especially their resourcefulness, a characteristic much seen in my own big, to-tea-on-Sundays family so typical of the northern mill towns.

Conway Street, Halifax, where I was born in 1904, amidst this band of relations, is today still a drab thoroughfare, paved with stone setts, its tiny back-to-back houses sheltering so many people that I now wonder how they can find space to move, let alone live individual lives. As a child I wasn't conscious of being engulfed by it all, but all the same I used to love to steal off up to the attic, push up the window in the roof and stand on a box looking out over the sea of dark-blue slates. Sometimes the industrial haze would vanish just when one thought it never could, to reveal a sky as fresh and colourful as I was told it always was at Blackpool.

This was hardly surprising as, for me, the annual pilgrimage to that queen of the northern coast represented the high spot of my small existence then. Although preoccupied with the constant struggle to keep the family, particularly my elder brother Arthur and myself, in clothes and food, my parents would usually manage to provide us with a holiday. This was mainly thanks to my impetuous father. When the summer holidays came round he would say, as he had said all through the year: 'We can't go away, we can't afford it'. Then, suddenly, he would burst in to announce: 'We're going to Blackpool!'

As I visualise my father, he looked rather as I am now, although he had a ruddier complexion and a rougher, more untidy appearance. This was deceptive, for even in the worst of our family's economic troubles he showed a lively wit that made him the immediate centre of attention in any company. One example of his wit I remember quite clearly. We were walking in the country one day when a hunt came by, in full scarlet and with a large pack of hounds. Quite twenty minutes later a solitary horseman rode past. My father cocked an eye towards him: 'One man's meet', he grinned.

My mother Margaret, small, dark-haired and home-loving, was of a very different nature from my father, quieter and more reserved. In later years, though she was quietly proud of my success, it would never occur to her to let me know this with a few words of praise or encouragement. On the contrary, she hid her feelings under a typically dour northern exterior. I well remember asking her if she'd listened to the start of a new programme series.

'Oh yes', she replied in an off-hand sort of way.

'Well, what did you think of it?'

After some deliberation she proffered generously, 'I expect you get stuck fast as to what to do next.'

This attitude stemmed from mother's strict upbringing, her own mother having been left a widow at thirty-nine with seven children to bring up, five of them daughters. Mother told me how the girls would bring home their wages and drop them into my grandmother's outstretched apron and how she would look at the collected pittances with an expression of resignation which said: 'How on earth are we going to manage?' None of her daughters dared to stay out after nine o'clock and, as the curfew hour approached, she would sit outside the house, watchful and challenging.

Of course, when I knew her, grandmother was not the martinet of those earlier days. One of my greatest joys was to go round to her house every Wednesday, baking day, when she would produce delicious flat cakes, sometimes known as oven-bottom cakes, and spread them thickly with butter. I would go off to eat mine in the living-room, with its dark mahogany sideboard and the horsehair sofa which always pricked my knees when I knelt on it. In a corner stood a 'whatnot' littered with trinkets, most of them labelled 'A Present from Blackpool' or 'A Present from Skegness' and including a pot pig—a souvenir from Cleethorpes.

I will never forget when I was detailed to take the news of my younger brother George's death to my grandmother. The sadness and the experience of seeing my mother and father in such trouble had started to react on me. Upset, and almost breathless, I told her what had happened and added: 'I'll never get over this, Gran'ma.' She put her arm round my shoulder, pulled me towards her and said, quietly and firmly: 'Ay, lad, but tha will.'

It was a lesson about life which was to stand me in good stead over the years during which I experienced more heartbreak such as my grandmother had already known. And troubles *were* more easily forgotten then, especially with the companionship of the rest of my mother's sisters.

One of the most amusing of them was Aunt Emma, a real Yorkshire lass whose most endearing qualities seemed to have been brought out by adversity. Her husband, Uncle Jim, was a dyer's labourer who spent as much time unemployed as he did working. They had thirteen children who brought them much pride and some pain. Only in later years was I to appreciate the staunch resilience of Aunt Emma's reply when one of her girls broke the news that she was pregnant. This was in the days when bloomers, long knickers with elastic at the knees, had replaced drawers, the split-between-the-legs combination-like garments worn by most women previously. In a tone of despair Aunt Emma passed off her wayward daughter's 'crime' with the words, 'Well, I wouldn't have cared, but you're the only one that's worn bloomers!'

Equally blunt, my Uncle Jim often proved a source of embarassment to those of his children who had 'gone up in the world'. One particular girl had married someone much better off than her parents, a staunch teetotaller who owned his own horse and trap. Thinking her mother and father would enjoy a day's outing from Halifax, the girl invited them for a run in the trap. After an early start they had covered quite a distance by midday—opening time for Jim. Still the pony went on, the driver giving no sign of a halt till, in desperation, Jim called out, 'This is the funniest horse I've ever come across. It stops neither to sup nor piddle.'

I was influenced and encouraged most by Aunt Sarah, my mother's eldest sister, who, although well into her fifties, could neither read nor write. As a girl, she had had the responsibility thrust upon her of helping to bring up her brothers and sisters, and was consequently left unmarried and without a formal education. But she adored listening to a good book—and I became her reader. Aunt Sarah's satisfaction with my reading seemed to me all the more valuable because of her dependence on me. When I came to a long word which baffled me, she would say understandingly: 'Never mind, lad; just say 'alifax and get over it!' Right to the end she never lost that mannerism which marks the millworker of Lancashire and Yorkshire—the exaggerated movement of the lips in framing words.

My father got on well with my mother's family, probably

because he was used to living amongst many—he had two brothers and four sisters. My mother tolerated the extraordinary hold these sisters undoubtedly had on him. He always visited them on Sunday mornings, a habit which he showed no disposition to break. 'Ahm gooin' round to see our lasses,' he would say, and my mother, to whom they were always 'your lasses', agreed uncomplainingly.

Aunt Sarana (Sarah Hannah) was the most impressive of them all. It would be no exaggeration to say that she ran the family. She was a grand organiser, a born controller, and the ideal person to have about when there was trouble, yet I was convinced that her main impulse was a longing to know what was going on within other people's four walls. Two of her sisters, Annie and Lizzie, lived with Sarana and her husband. The fourth sister, Aunt Jinney, nearest to my father as a wit, married and moved away to the Midlands. Her children had strong Birmingham accents—but nevertheless their speech was praised by the Yorkshire Pickles family!

My father's two brothers, Isaac and Walter, were like him, stonemasons in the family building business. With his shiny face, bald head and general well preserved appearance, Isaac was the complete prosperous businessman; the successful Yorkshireman who owed it to nobody but himself. Unknowingly, by his actions in founding his own firm and stepping out of the backstreet rut, he helped to focus my own feelings and aims.

I believe I profited too in an unexpected way from such close contact with so many relations in those early days in Halifax, a tough town breeding rather a stubborn, insular people. I found a depressing narrowness of outlook there, and resented my family's unquestioning judgement that everything they did was right and anything to the contrary was to be condemned. People who had coffee for breakfast were peculiar and not to be trusted, while the folk living on the other side of North Bridge had none of our earthy qualities! Bradford, eight miles away, was another world which could not, therefore, be a desirable place. In fact, this somewhat staid town was almost represented as sin city. The good citizens were supposedly out for all they could get, although appearances had to be kept up. We all heard the tale of the watch committee faced with a naughty film, whose chairman turned to his fellow members with relish after the run through and said, 'I'll tell you what, we'll see it just once more, then we'll ban it'!

Although I never visited Bradford until I was grown up, as I became older it became apparent to me, that there was something bigger than Halifax, a wider world in which minds could broaden—in short, a really expansive pond in which little frogs weren't made to feel much bigger than their actual size. It seemed to me that the first step away was to find a job, especially one to which my mother would not object in the difficult war years whilst father was away fighting. Presently I managed to persuade her that something suitable could be given a try, and I was duly engaged, half-time, as errand boy at Mitchell's, a local ladies' and gents' outfitters. Despite bouts of boredom and frustration over the more mundane side of shop work, I enjoyed delivering parcels to parts of my home-town never before seen. Indeed, so assiduous was I at carrying out my duties that I was soon promoted to performing trusted tasks for Mr Mitchell himself, and when the time came for me to leave school at thirteen I was happy to be taken on the full-time staff.

My satisfaction with being a salesman did not last long, however. Although no scholar—to be frank, I hated school and was delighted to leave—I was still an avid reader. Now I was borrowing volumes of poetry and plays from the public library, and had discovered Shelley, Keats, Galsworthy and Shaw. Dreams I had and wonderful moments of self-deception when I saw myself as a great actor. Alongside the

old, ornate Theatre Royal ran a dimly lit passage where the
queue formed for the pit stalls and which also led to the stage
door. In the evenings I waited for actors to appear and
watched them hurrying through the passage and past the
line of people. Then, pulling up my coat collar, I followed,
walking quickly, urgently, and wondering if those people
were thinking I was an actor and hoping to heaven they
were. If an actor had stopped to speak to me I should very
likely have been speechless and completely overcome, for I
looked upon these men and women of the plays as people
from another world, a divine fairyland where folk were
perfect and where all human relationships were on the grand
scale.

One day, whilst still at Mitchell's, I was spellbound to see
the great actor Fred Terry coming into the shop, confident,
serene and just as I had seen him to be in *The Scarlet Pimpernel*
at the Royal. I stared at this wonderful creature and then
glanced all over the shop to see how people would react.
Perhaps I expected a deferential bow or something of equal
tribute from every member of the staff and each customer, but
nothing happened. They all carried on with their jobs as if
he were Bert Smith of High Street, Halifax. Then one of
the assistants stepped forward. 'Yes, sir', he said brightly.
'What can we . . .?' I waited, in suspense, to hear that
wonderful voice. Terry spoke: 'I want some underpants',
he said.

I was still staring. But gradually the words sank in.
Underpants! Fred Terry buying underpants! Fred Terry
wearing underpants! It was one of the greatest shocks of my
youth.

Even after that incident, however, my reverence for the
great actors and actresses who found their way to Halifax did
not waver. In spite of the mental pedestal I reserved for
actors I still felt sure they would be glad to be playing

Halifax, and I was sorry for them when they left for theatres at places like Bradford or Burnley. Halifax was still my world and I took it for granted it would be theirs, too.

My stage ambitions were not limited to hero worship and I was gradually finding my feet as an entertainer at Sunday School concerts. My act was recitations. People invited me to other Sunday Schools and every week found me in some out-of-the-way part of Halifax I had never seen before, not even on my rounds for Mitchell's.

At one of these concerts, after I had given my turn, a man stepped forward and announced: 'And now—I'm sure Wilfred wouldn't mind if *I* do a recitation.' To my amazement he started on a piece entitled 'On t'Desert', by Corporal R. E. I was desperate to tell him immediately that Corporal R. E. was my father, of the whole history of that piece of writing and of my father's Service life. Like thousands of others, he found the Army a happy hunting ground for funny stories, and again and again would have us all doubled up laughing at his tales. He was as popular among his Army pals as he had always been at the club in Halifax, and up to the time nearing his death he went to the annual reunions in Manchester. Not all that long ago, an old soldier turned up in Manchester where I was playing and shook my hand warmly. 'And how's thi Dad?' he asked.

'I'm afraid he's dead', I said. Then he told me how much he'd enjoyed the show, but added: 'If tha doesn't mind me sayin' it, tha'rt not so funny as thi father!' I might have known that would come!

His letters from the front were painstakingly done and could have been placed alongside the best of the light writing that was coming from the trenches during World War I. They were full of the broad, unsophisticated humour so characteristic of those times, and my brother Arthur was so sure of their quality that he forwarded them to the *Yorkshire*

Weekly Post in which they duly appeared under the hastily coined by-line 'By Corporal R. E.'

Here is a bit from 'In Hospital' where he described first seeing the doctor and then eventually arriving at the hospital itself.

Well, I managed to get inside at last, an' by gum it were a fine place. I were full o' beds, an' t'floor were nicely polished, an' I noticed 'ut it smelled nice an' warm. About half o' t' beds were full (course they nobbut hold one), some were asleep, an' some were wakken. Then I saw a woman wi' a long white pinny on, an' a long white table cover on her head. I don't know what she put it theer for—happen so as she'd know where to find it at tea time. When she saw me i' t'doorway, she come up to me as quiet as a mouse, an' she asked me what I ailed, and she spoke that quiet I thought she were afraid of her husband coppin' us! Well, believe me, as soon as I told her, she shoved a long glass tube i' my mouth an' then she got hold o' my wrist. Well, we stood like this for a bit, an' I were beginning to feel a bit nervous wi' this glass thing in my mouth an' her hold o' my wrist. I'd nobbut one hand at liberty, so I put that i' my pocket an' stuck to my brass, for there were nobbut eightpence between me an' starvation. Well, she pulled this thing out o' my mouth, an' stared at it as though I'd bitten some off, an' then she looked at me an' said: 'you're a hundred and one'.

'Nay, Missus', I says. 'I know I've aged since I come in here, but I'm not half that yet.'

She laughed and says: 'You funny man. I've taken your temperature.' I don't know what she meant but she hadn't gotten my eightpence for that were i' my hand. Well, wi' big shifts and little 'uns I got into bed. First one come, then another, an' then t'doctor come, an' put rubber tubes in his ears like one o' them old fashioned talking machines they used to have at t'fair. When I'd gotten rid of him, a woman come to me (I think she were a visitor) an' she offered me some paper an' envelopes, an' said would I like to write home? 'Why, Missus', I says, 'don't yo' think I stand much chance o' seein' 'em again?' I'll be hanged if I weren't gettin' a bit scared.

'Well,' thinks I, 'they're a long time bringing me summat to eat. They've given me nowt yet. It's been all takin'—they've tekken my perticklers, my religion, my temperature an' my clothes; I've nobbut my life left, an' that feels very uncertain here, for they walk about that quiet, an' talk that low, while you can never tell what they're schemin.'

Well, I don't know how I slept, I were that hungry, but when I wakkened, they were buzin' about wi' t'breakfasts to everybody but me. I got tired o' watching 'em go past me, so I says: 'Have yo' fergetten me?'

She says: 'No, Corporal, we are going to give you X-rays.'

'Well, bring it up sharp,' I says, 'for I'm famished.'

My father's 'literary' talent was an instinctive one which he never bothered to pursue when he returned to his life as a stonemason. I joined him in the business, all the time continuing to read and write, to absorb material with which to conquer my brave new world. Whilst brick-laying and building prevented me from becoming bored, I was continually reminded of that narrowness of outlook I had noticed before, and my waning respect for the small-town Napoleons dropped still further. Although I was not convinced where my road lay, I had a notion that my love of books and good writing and, not least, of the stage, might be signposts.

Then, when I was fourteen, the unbelievable happened. One day I'd spent several weeks' savings in one buy—a collection of Shakespeare's works, which cost me five shillings—and that night I sat by the hearth reading part of it to my mother. Suddenly she got up and said: 'I think you'd better 'ave some lessons in acting, lad.' Lessons in acting! I had never thought we would be able to afford it. But here was my mother actually suggesting it.

The Reverend Henry Ironmonger had a reputation in Halifax as a successful teacher of elocution and I had heard his marathon recitations of Dickens' *A Christmas Carol* long before that winter evening when I became one of his pupils. A diminutive, dapper Congregationalist minister, he ran classes in his home. About a dozen young people made up my class and we were set to recite such poems as 'Not Understood', 'The Highwayman' and 'The Revenge'.

The only things I failed to absorb from Mr Ironmonger's teaching were those I rejected as wrong. I thought he had rather an old-fashioned style (how I disliked that swinging of arms, those overdone gestures). Surely the interpretation should come from the voice. I was convinced it should and I wonder now how much this had to do with the radio technique I was to develop years afterwards.

I was now ruled by a great ambition to be a success on the stage. My best friend at the time never stopped pulling me up for my Yorkshire accent which he tried to correct. As it was to become one of the main characteristics in the process of making my way, it is probably as well I did not take his criticism to heart.

When I was eighteen I joined an amateur dramatic society. It was a very young group; the King Cross Amateur Dramatic Society, which had yet to give its first production. We finally settled on a play far above the level of our competence, *Julius Caesar*, in which I was to be Brutus. I learned the whole part in two days, an achievement of which even the thought upsets me now. Three members of that inexperienced group eventually became professional actors.

One was a handsome lad with a distinctive personality. I knew him well because he had been to school at Rishworth with my brother Arthur; our mutual interest in the theatre brought us together, and I used to slip into his father's shop where we would talk about acting and plays and actors and playwrights for hours on end. We would be discussing the possibilities of *Hamlet* or *Twelfth Night* when a customer would enter. My friend would contort his face into an expression of frustration and rebellion, continue the discussion for a moment or two longer and then break off to serve a

25

tie or shirt. He hated it all. Such was the early single-mindedness of Eric Portman.

I soon got my first glimpse behind the scenes of a real theatre. A young and brilliant actor called Henry Baynton brought his company to Halifax to perform Shakespeare's plays. This man, who was trained at the Benson School, accomplished something which astounded everybody with an interest in the stage. He packed the Theatre Royal from floor to ceiling and 'house full' notices had to be posted outside. For *Julius Caesar* he brought in local amateurs to play the crowd; and I saw to it that I was one of those selected. To make the evening memorable, Baynton patted me on the head as he walked through the 'crowd' as Brutus. I walked on air for days.

Eric Portman also fell under Baynton's spell, to such an extent that he resolved to go with the company when it moved on to conquer other towns. When the players returned to Halifax some months later the young Portman was taking important parts and his name was included on the posters advertising the show. My brother and I decided to meet him to talk over old times. As Arthur and I waited, we talked about Eric and his acting and exchanged theories about what improvement he might have made under Baynton. I noticed a figure coming towards us wearing a wide-brimmed Homburg hat pulled well down over the forehead, and a heavy gorilla-shouldered overcoat. As the man drew close I joked loudly to Arthur: 'Here he is'.

We both laughed. But it was indeed Eric! He was now the complete actor and, just as I had once walked down the queue in the half-light hoping they would take me for an actor, Eric, I thought, was now carrying off a development of that form of exhibitionism, pretending to himself that he was a stranger playing in a strange land. He even asked us the way to St James' Road, one of the main streets of Halifax!

26

To me, Eric was the man with the torch. He had started out and in doing so had shown me the way. I persevered with my acting and spent night after night learning lines, rehearsing scenes from plays that ranged from Shakespeare to the light efforts of minor playwrights of the day. Every night as I tramped slowly homewards through the silent streets, past the windows of scores of little houses, I was thinking of stage techniques and of great roles I was bursting to play. . . .

2 MABEL

The old adage that behind every successful man there is a strong woman could not be more true in my case. I can honestly say that Mabel, my business advisor as well as my wife, has contributed as much to my career as she has in providing a happy family home. Constant companions for the last forty-seven years, like all close couples we have our occasional tiffs but the pleasure we've always gained from each other's company still shows. A year or so ago, for instance, when we'd been married forty years, we passed a group of young girls waiting outside the house of a pop star in London's Harley Street. Recognising me from television appearances, one of the girls exclaimed, 'Oh it's Wilfred Pickles', then turning to Mabel on my arm she asked brightly 'And are you his bird?'

Whilst I'm a firm believer that man can shape his own ends by his own efforts I also believe that there is some ultimate guiding force which controls our destiny. Or how else were the set of circumstances contrived which brought about my marriage and eventual career? Just as I was starting to make a name for myself in Halifax dramatic circles, my father was offered a post as manager of a building company in Southport which he decided was an opportunity not to be missed. At first I stayed behind, until the strain of working in the building trade all day and acting all night began to take its toll. Very soon it became obvious that I needed a rest if a complete breakdown were to be avoided, so I gave up my job, decided to forget acting aspirations, at least for the time being, and went to join my parents in Lancashire.

The quietness and fresh sea breezes of Southport were a real tonic and in next to no time I was feeling in fine form. Before I had time to become bored I made the aquaintance of Arthur Belt, one-time producer with the Manchester Repertory Company, who told me he was putting on a play at the local church. Belt soon explained that he was disappointed with the young man playing the juvenile lead and, when he knew of my interest, suggested that I should go to a rehearsal and show what I was worth.

The day I turned up at the church hall Belt lost no time in introducing me to the cast. I immediately forgot all their names, however, as my eyes were fixed on a girl with glistening auburn hair. Only when she disappeared did my mind turn back to Belt to hear him asking me to read through the juvenile lead. As I went through the lines quite easily, I could see Belt was overjoyed. I was dying to act with this group but also thought it would be unsportsmanlike to displace the lad who had been rehearsing the part for several weeks. As soon as I was able to corner the producer on his own, I told him of my decision. He was rather disgruntled, but the rest of the cast, to whom the news soon spread, were evidently relieved. Soon they were all chattering happily together—and in their midst was the girl with the auburn hair. I had heard Belt address her as Mabel, but for the life of me I couldn't remember her surname.

Long after we had all dispersed, I was still urgently searching my memory for the name and it suddenly occurred to me that the most convenient way of finding out was to go down the road and look at one of the bill posters advertising the show. I walked around scrutinizing the hoardings until I came across the poster I wanted. Mabel . . . Mabel . . .

Mabel . . . I was thinking. Then I saw it—Mabel Myers-cough.

The next move was to learn where she lived, so I approached Belt as casually as possible and simply asked him for the Myerscoughs' address. The following morning, a Sunday, found me strolling past the Myerscoughs' house in the hope of seeing this girl Mabel. Up and down I went several times like a policeman on his beat, sometimes pretending to be quite purposeful and in a hurry to get somewhere although, in fact, I merely went to the corner of the road before doubling back. Fortunately, just before my behaviour excited suspicion, I was spotted by John, Mabel's youngest brother, who came to the door and called: 'Are you looking for me?' Although in a vague way I had wanted to be hailed by the Myerscoughs I was taken aback now that it had happened, so I swallowed my pride, disguised my nervousness, and lied 'Yes'.

John then invited me in, introducing me to the rest of the family. Aware that an immediate explanation was expected I told them hopefully, but not very confidently, that I had been wondering if the society would care for me to give a hand with the make-up for the play. That was the signal for an animated exchange about the show and I soon realised that all the family were in on it in some way or other. I recognised both Mabel's brothers as the men who were looking after the lighting and the stage management at the hall, and I had also seen her father at the rehearsal, looking like a colonel, erect and handsome with his white moustache. From this first meeting there grew up a deep friendship which became ever stronger until Mabel's father died in 1946. He might have been my own father, he was so interested in my welfare and ambitions.

What impressed me was the contrast between Mabel's family and my own. I had been brought up to regard the hours of eight to five as exclusively working hours, just as

Monday to Friday was a working period, and there was to be no thought of pleasure until Saturday. But this did not apply in the Myerscoughs' home. They were accustomed to entertaining and all of them had been connected with the stage, even Mabel's uncles and aunts. Their talk pleased me. It had a wide range and was full of the sort of shop-talk I imagined actors indulged in when they got together away from the theatre. It was an enriching experience for me just to be among these people who talked easily and enthusiastically about all the things that interested me and who had learned so much about drama and the art of entertainment.

Although our families had such different backgrounds and approaches to life, Mabel and I were delighted to find that they got on so well together, just as we did. As my friendship with Mabel developed, she became convinced of my acting ability and never gave up encouraging me to stick to my ambitions. After that second meeting in her home, hardly an evening passed that did not find us together, and we saw every play within reach. We went regularly to the Opera House in Southport and booked for every new show at the Liverpool Playhouse.

Mabel, who was born in Liverpool, had long been a devotee of the outstanding Liverpool Repertory Company, whose little theatre was as intimate as a beehive and the scene of as much devoted work. There, in Williamson Square, right in the very heart of the commercial metropolis of the north, art thrived on half an acre. And the man who nurtured it was in his way a genius—William Armstrong, the director. He was a discerning man who knew a good play and who had extraordinary ability to spot latent talent. In the company at this time were Robert Donat, Marjorie Fielding, Diana Wynyard, and Wyndham Goldie.

I looked forward to our Saturday evenings in Liverpool and if anybody had asked me at this time, 'Are yer coortin'?'

31

I would have answered with a very definite 'Yes'. Indeed, within four months of our first meeting, Mabel and I were engaged. We both knew that, although we shared many common interests, our personalities were completely different. But, more important, we had seen how complementary were those personalities. Mabel was practical, her feet were firmly planted on the ground and she looked much further ahead than I did. She invariably saw the sensible way, which so rarely occurred to me because my head was in the clouds. 'You're a dreamer, an idealist. I'll have to look after you', Mabel once said.

It was during our engagement that her practical vision more or less set me on the road to a career I had not planned. One weekend, after we had seen a particularly moving show in Liverpool, I decided that I would like to join the Liverpool Repertory Company.

'I wouldn't dash into it. I think you would be better on the radio', Mabel replied. 'There's a real opportunity there and until you've seen what the chances are of getting into it, I should forget about the Rep.' She said she was in no way questioning my abilities as a stage actor, but she was convinced I had a technique that was peculiarly suited to broadcasting. 'You can play two or three parts in one play, like the other night when you read both the old man's and the young woman's parts and that sort of thing can be done so well on the air. Don't you think it's worth trying?'

It was all very novel to me but I had to admit that there was something in what she had said. From that moment I have never regretted taking her advice. She has a gift for seeing things on her horizon before they have reached the level of my feet. Mabel has always run the business side of our affairs. She keeps the books, pays all the bills, deals with the bank manager and argues with the accountants. And, perhaps more important, she has always used her acute judgement to make sure that I've never been associated with

The typical Pickles pose: a recent portrait taken in his London flat (*TV Times*)

(left) Wilfred and Mabel take a stroll down memory lane on a return visit to Halifax where they looked up his birthplace, 24 Conway Street (*Halifax Evening Courier*)

(right) and called in on his old school (*Halifax Evening Courier*)

anything which might upset my public. If I was invited to appear in a charity concert, for instance, Mabel would always check the rest of the bill and, should there be a comic who was known for his smutty stories, she would suggest that I didn't accept as she knew that my simple, homely humour would mean nothing by contrast.

Less than a year after our engagement, we decided to get married. We made our home in Southport, slipping for a few months into the suburban grooves: regular working hours, a spick-and-span home, over-the-garden-wall discussions with our neighbours, evening walks round the neat rows of houses on balmy summer evenings. I was still working with my father laying bricks—and hating it even more than ever. There was an undercurrent of revolt in my mind. I had made no serious effort to move into the professional theatre, but the longing was still there. One day, I felt sure, I would have to strike out and break new ground, meet new people and be absolutely independent of the family.

Very soon, however, I had to establish other priorities as Mabel became pregnant. We were delighted at the prospect of becoming parents. Then, shortly afterwards, we had our first setback. Mabel collapsed in the bedroom. I sent for the doctor, knowing that something must be wrong with the baby. But the doctor was not sure. In fact, he had not the remotest idea what the trouble was, and even went so far as to suggest that we should go to the infirmary as the pain might be caused by appendicitis.

The next day I drove Mabel to Liverpool, where we were told that something *had* gone wrong with the pregnancy and that she would have to be operated on the same night. I stayed on at the hospital, waiting to hear how the operation had gone, and it was a tremendous relief when a nurse came down the corridor to tell me that all seemed well. It was only then I learned that Mabel might easily have bled to death. We had lost the child, but she was safe and doing well.

On 20 August in the following year, however, we had the greatest thrill of our lives when our son, David, was born. Naturally, we stayed at home even more now, and most evenings we would hold play-reading sessions. I still delighted in reading aloud, although I was so convinced that the family would think me a terrible bore that I would hide the books away if any of them came round to see us unexpectedly.

All too soon it seemed, our happy, close-knit existence was disturbed by two tragic events—the outbreak of war and, for us, an even more heartbreaking personal disaster. I was now working for the BBC in Manchester, and one evening I received a telephone message from Mabel to say that David had suddenly been taken ill and was vomiting. By the time I got home he was fairly bright but obviously still unwell, and we decided to send for the doctor, even though it was very late. On examining David, the doctor was somewhat perturbed because his temperature was so high. Even when he called again the next day he still could not get the temperature down.

As we were increasingly concerned, Mabel suggested we might do better with a second opinion. It was late in the evening of the second day of David's illness when the specialist arrived. I still remember very clearly how David's bedroom door opened and the two doctors came slowly down the stairs and said they would like a word with us. Then came those awful words: 'I suspect your boy has contracted infantile paralysis.'

The doctor suggested that David be moved immediately to Salford Infirmary where he could be placed in an iron lung and have constant, specialised supervision. The thought of our only child being taken away alarmed us, but we had to make an immediate decision and so agreed. Mabel and I felt it was strange that the doctors suspected David of being very ill, for he was in reasonably high spirits and quite talkative, though we had noticed that his voice had become slightly metallic.

It was two o'clock in the morning when the ambulance arrived. David, still quite conscious, did not like it at all, but we managed to persuade him, as the ambulance men wrapped him in a red blanket, that it was only for a day, and he was happier when I climbed into the ambulance alongside him. I thought it was better for Mabel not to join us on that journey and I knew that was the right course to have taken when I saw David being put into bed in one of the wards. As I stood there, a doctor whispered: 'Your boy is very ill, you know. I think it would be better if you went home. I'm afraid you can't do any good here.'

David had no idea what time of day it was as he looked up and said to me: 'You ought to be going, Dad—or you'll be late for the BBC.'

That night, Mabel and I lay awake worrying about David and when we went to see him a few hours later, we had a further grave disappointment: he was unconscious. The doctor allowed us to stay on by his bedside, although, presently, a nursing sister came along and advised us, with genuine concern, to go home and have some food and rest.

Mabel had changed even in appearance. She was like a marble statue. Her face was pale and I noticed her hands were trembling. When I spoke to her she did not hear me. It was the first of November, a cold grey day, and at five o'clock in the morning, not long after we had dozed off for the first time, there came the most ominous knock I have ever heard. It was our neighbour whose telephone number I had given at the hospital. I was wanted. Nervously, I picked up the receiver, to hear a voice at the other end say: 'I'm very sorry to tell you that your little boy has just passed away.'

There was an awful silence. I have never known just what my feelings were in those chilling moments. All I recall is that I knew I had to go back into our home and tell Mabel.

If only she could have cried when I gave the dreadful news it would have been so much better for her. But she remained taut, filled with tears she could not shed. Inadequately, all I could do was offer to make her a cup of tea.

Then the thought flashed through my mind that many of David's clothes and toys were lying scattered about the house and that they would be painful reminders to Mabel as long as we had them, so I did something I could never do now in similar circumstances. I went all over the house, carefully gathering together all David's things; his shoes, his books, his tin soldiers. Collecting them into a bundle, I wrapped them up in a sheet which I hid in a shed behind the house. And at nine o'clock, just four hours after we had heard of David's death, I telephoned the health authorities and asked them to collect the bundle.

'But it's not an infectious disease', said an official.

'I know, but please treat it as if it were', I said. The bundle was duly collected and Mabel was spared a lot of painful reminders.

Again I experienced the wonderful friendliness of ordinary folk, and their unsparing determination to share the burdens of a great personal tragedy. People rallied round; relatives, friends and neighbours did all they could to ease our path in those days of grief.

Mabel faced up to the greatest tragedy of her life with real stoicism, and, whereas many women would have gone under, she kept up a brave front. It is said that time is a great healer, but even now Mabel cannot talk about those four terrible days which left us without our only son and changed our lives so much.

From that moment on we were rarely apart, except when I was working, and I'm afraid that my absences became all the more inevitable as my BBC career blossomed. Mabel experienced a very lonely spell, especially when I started working weekends too. I know that many a wife would have declared: 'Chuck it! We're not sacrificing home life for it', but Mabel showed no signs of jibbing and never complained. On the contrary she looked well ahead and, whenever I brought the subject up, would say: 'There'll be a settled job eventually.'

As usual she proved to be right and, as my own fame grew, in broadcasting and on the stage, I made sure that she was a part of it. We worked happily together in pantomime and the 'straight' theatre before the overwhelming success of *Have a Go* when the words 'Give 'im the money, Mabel' became almost as well known as the theme song. Ever-adaptable, Mabel moved with ease from thinking up the questions for *Have a Go* to joining in the fun of the TV programme *Ask Pickles*, where we granted all sorts of unusual requests—an idea, incidentally, which has been used time and again since in such shows as *Ask Aspel* and *Jim'll Fix It*.

Mabel is younger than I am, and by jove she looks it! Today, at an age when many people have slowed down considerably, she is as active as ever, happily accompanying me at all times, even if it means getting up at 6 am to catch an early train to the north, doing a day's work and not getting back till midnight. Theatrical digs are still as much home to her as any luxury hotel. I still thank my lucky stars in finding a co-star who is also cook-housekeeper, a lasting love who is, above all, a good friend, and someone with a business brain to match a shapely ankle. Long may there continue to be good reasons for me to say 'Give 'im the money Mabel'.

3   LIFE WITH 'AUNTIE'

Broadcasting has certainly seen some changes over the years, Television, with all its increasingly sophisticated techniques —though not necessarily better programmes —has, of course. made the greatest impact, but much has altered in radio too. When I first started there was no such amazing process as video-tape, a fact which today's television-age children would find hard to grasp as they unquestioningly watch *Match of the Day* with all the wonders of instant-replay and similar feats. Indeed, in the early days of radio virtually everything went out live, so that every fluffed line, every unavoidable cough was heard over the air.

Also, there were far fewer backroom boys then and the announcer or interviewer often doubled as technician, pressing buttons and pulling switches to start or end programmes, rather like the DJs and 'open-line' broadcasters in some cases today. One particular instance when someone failed to take the right action in time has always amused me. This was after an interview with a bishop for the morning religious slot. The talk had gone quite well in rehearsal, if a little too slow for the time allowed, and the interviewer had had to ask the clergyman to speed up his delivery so as not to over-run. After the closing words, 'And one day we shall all meet in heaven', the bishop asked quickly, 'I don't think I was too long was I?' Unprepared for this continued speech, the announcer flicked the cut-out switch but was too late to prevent a couple of unscripted words going out, with the result that the bishop appeared to have said, 'And one day we shall all meet in heaven, I don't think'!

Even when recordings were used for regular short pieces there was still much room for error. Whether the religious broadcasts were particularly susceptible or whether the very nature of the material often contributed to unwanted effects, for some reason, there is a fund of instructive anecdotes connected with religious broadcasting. For instance, the *Lift Up Your Hearts* programme used to be recorded on an ordinary disc, thus enabling the presenter to absent himself for what he knew to be a set period of time. On one occasion he was a minute or so late in returning, the record came to an end and the needle stuck on the final groove playing over and over again the phrase 'For Christ's Sake, Amen', 'For Christ's Sake Amen', 'For Christ's Sake . . .'.

Being such a mammoth organisation and controlling so much output, the BBC can't help but be the butt of many comedians, practical jokers and even, inadvertently, score points against itself. On one occasion, for instance, some bright spark pointed out that it looked disrespectful to have details of the morning service sandwiched between a pop group and a recital in the *Radio Times*. So it was decided to elaborate on the content of the service on another page. Thus the entry apparently read 'The ten commandments: "Thou shalt not commit adultery". For further details, see page 14!'

Much has changed too in the way of style and presentation. In radio's early days music hall was still a strong force and stand-up comics were almost as common on the air as on the halls. Now, of course, apart from spasmodic revivals and watered-down TV reconstructions such as *The Good Old Days*, music hall is virtually dead. The straight theatre plays to empty houses—out of three successful theatres in Halifax in my youth, not one remains—and even the cinema has failed to compete with the almost non-stop entertainment offered by television. Consequently, the old-fashioned performers, who were taught to project to fill vast buildings, the comedians forced to buttonhole their audience with loud delivery, are now creatures of the past, or, if not, then they are most certainly out of work. The natural style has taken over both radio and TV, so casual, in fact, that viewers have been known to fall asleep in front of the weather man, a habit not solely caused by the lateness of the hour.

And as the style of playing to an audience has changed, so too has the humour. Variety clubs, the supposed modern equivalent of the music halls, suffer from what can only be called tele-conditioning, in that the audience will pay only to see the big names known to them through TV spectaculars and can be dismissive of acts which don't measure up to what they are used to 'on the box'. Sandy Powell, that great old campaigner, told me how he died a death in trying to make the transition from music hall to the clubs. His act was a hilarious send-up of ventriloquists, moving his lips all the time, using an uncoordinated dummy. After a somewhat lukewarm reception, he heard one lady member of the audience complain to another, 'I don't think he's a patch on Arthur Worsley'.

Music is, of course, one of the staples of clubland entertainment, but even in this area there are unforeseen pitfalls. Reg Dixon, the comedian famed for his *Confidentially* theme tune, realised that he had lost his audience half way through his allotted span, so cut the act short and afterwards asked the manager what had gone wrong.

'O, I should have warned you' he replied cheerfully. 'That always happens when the hot pies come!'

But we really can't blame that on the popularity of those so-called TV dinners, snacks to eat on a tray while tele-viewing. Or can we?

The wheel has certainly come full circle with a vengeance as regards radio drama too, particularly the regional productions, for though the quality of plays on BBC has always been high, there was not always the money to afford top-class actors, so that in some cases the 'natural' approach was all too easily achieved. Today there is a BBC repertory company, actors and actresses employed on a fixed salary like other employees, taking all parts, from King Lear to a game-keeper, in their stride and for the same reward. But regional drama in the thirties relied mainly on amateurs, drawing its performers from all walks of life—accountants and mill-workers who had a full-time job during the day, worked for the BBC in the evenings. In this way it could take three evenings, from seven to ten o'clock each night, to produce a simple one-act play.

Despite the frequently poor performances, I was a regular listener in those early days when my own dramatic ambitions were still more or less unfulfilled. How well I remember one particular night, when Mabel and I were reading *Man and Superman*, when I suddenly remembered there was a play on the air. As the production was slow and not particularly well acted, Mabel said in exasperation: 'Oh, let's have it off and get back to our own play.' Then she continued indignantly, 'Why don't you have that shot at the BBC, as I've kept telling you? If they'll stand for that, they'll stand for you!'

Her remark caught my imagination so much that I sat down straightaway and framed a carefully worded letter to the BBC in Manchester, asking if they would 'kindly grant me an audition'. I listed the parts I had played and named the amateur societies I had been associated with.

So confident were we of a satisfactory reply that, next evening, we worked out a plan for the readings I would give when the BBC offered me a test. Something from Shake-peare would be expected and I decided on a soliloquy from *Hamlet*. This was to be followed by a speech from St John Ervine's *The Ship*, a few passages from Sean O'Casey's plays, some poetry and a bit of North-Country dialect in verse. Each night I rehearsed my set pieces, with Mabel as critic. For actuality, we put out the lights, except a reading lamp and Mabel judged my performance only on what she heard.

Then, one morning, came the invitation we had been waiting for: 'Broadcasting House, Manchester—4 pm Tuesday'. It left enough time to put the final polish to my readings, but those days seemed like a month. Already I was feeling that broadcasting was the one thing I really wanted to do and, with Mabel also set on the idea, I sensed the importance of the occasion for both of us.

On the day, arriving at the unprepossessing north regional headquarters in Piccadilly, Manchester, I left Mabel in the car, and entered. At least, I almost did, for a big commissionaire, one of the ex-sergeant-major types the Corporation seems to collect, halted me with: 'What's your business?' To me, the BBC seemed shrouded in mystery and I was so impressed by its power over so many people that I already felt desperately insignificant. My reception left me feeling smaller still. The bullying commissionaire ushered me unceremoniously into a thickly matted waiting-room where several others sat around, sharing a glum silence. Excitement was probably responsible for the unsociable atmosphere, but wasn't it also an unspoken terror of some secreted microphone which would blazen the least sound, the quietest, most personal remark, throughout this building—and possibly outside to listening millions?

It was like a dentist's waiting-room, so it came as a great relief when my name was called out by a young woman who led me to a studio and placed me about two feet from a suspended microphone. 'Right, you can begin now', she said.

I took in the room at a glance—the bareness, the thick, fitted carpet in fawn, and the clock on the wall above the door with a prominent seconds finger moving in silence.

Several chairs stood about, carelessly placed. The walls even looked soundproof and for a moment I had a fleeting vision of a padded cell. I felt just as lonely and isolated as if I had been in one. Nobody appeared to be ready to listen. I had no clue as to how much I was expected to read. It was like some surrealist joke.

I ran through my repertoire as rehearsed. Then the attractive young lady reappeared, told me to hold on, went away and then put her head round the door to ask: 'Can you do anything else?' Triumphantly, I leapt into the Sean O'Casey.

I had been inside about twenty minutes and, as I rushed outside to meet Mabel, she called from the car: 'How've you gone on?'

'I haven't the remotest idea', I replied. 'I've only seen a girl.'

During the next week or so we literally waited on the doorstep for the postman. On the tenth day we were rewarded by the arrival of a postcard signed by the head of the north regional drama department, to say my audition had been successful and that my name was now included on the department's list of players. Within a month there was a further communication offering me my first part. It was only four lines, but it was a start. I had earned money—three guineas—from broadcasting for the first time. And in the months that followed more work than I had dreamed possible came from the BBC, with my first leading part being that of the steel magnate John Wilkinson in *The Wilkinsons*, who aged from eighteen to seventy-plus during the play.

The BBC was now so much a part of my life that I had to keep a separate diary for my broadcasting engagements, many of them in *Children's Hour*, where I first met my lifelong friend Violet Carson now, as previously mentioned, almost taken over by the role of Ena Sharples but, as ever, a marvellous pianist and a great ally. It was Vi who was really responsible for my breaking into variety when she told the then regional head, David Porter, 'Why keep sending to London for folks to play these parts while all the time there's somebody on your own doorstep who can do the job equally well.' She then escorted me over to Porter who gave me the job. David Porter taught me one of the most important truths of our business. I learned from him that you can go on the air with one good act in a show like *Music Hall* and become well enough liked to be asked to play again, but that it is dangerous to be too eager to accept. The public are all too ready to say: 'He used to be all right, but he's no good now.' They forget the good and remember the bad. And it's perhaps relevant to mention at this point the advice given me, when I was already established, by Billy Danvers, the old music-hall comedian. 'You're doing very well now,' he said 'but the day will come when they will give you the bird, and I want you to answer back, "Yes, you're quite right," then tap your pocket and say "but you're too late".'

I'm delighted to say that I've never yet had to resort to such oneupmanship, although there were times in the early days when to have been able to utter such a retort would have pleased me no end. My relationship with the BBC, however, has on the whole been a happy one, and quite early on work began to fall into my lap without any real effort on my part to attract it. Perhaps my biggest break came when I was offered the job of northern holiday relief announcer, although as before it didn't come without the obligatory voice test. So once again I practised reading to Mabel at home. I 'announced' programmes from the *Radio Times* and listened closely, critically, to the London announcers, Stuart Hibberd and David Lloyd James, at every opportunity. Soon, I found myself slipping into their style of using the long 'a', saying 'pahst', instead of 'past'. But I didn't like it. If I was employed as a north regional announcer, why not use my own voice.

Mabel agreed. 'You might get a perfect imitation of those

fellows, but if you're going to be individual, you ought to do what's never been done before—speak like a North Country-man!' This seemed strange coming from one who is quite incapable of speaking even one word of dialect.

Although I knew I would be allowed to prepare my own imaginary programme introductions for this audition, I had a feeling that, to test me out adequately, they would thrust something at me that I had not seen before. They did. I had been prepared for foreign language announcements and it was here that the smattering of French I picked up at night school as a youth came in useful. I had also managed to accustom my ears to spoken French by listening to the radio which introduced me, too, to the pronunciation of Italian musical terms. When I went up to the mike in that empty studio, I felt determined to overcome anything that was put in front of me. I negotiated my announcements of French, German and Italian musical pieces fairly well; then came trouble!

I was handed a French novel to read. I knew it was beyond me, for this was a far cry from the short announcements of a few familiar words; but I also realised the best thing was to wade into it. That was easier to plan than to accomplish, and I soon stumbled awkwardly, sounding an 'h' where it should have been silent, exaggerating the acute accent, and floundering over the liaison between words.

Imagine my relief when the two 'judges' stepped out of the listening-room with broad grins on their faces and said 'Well, that's fine. We'd like you to start.' They admitted that they hadn't been able to understand a word of the novel from the way I read it, but apparently my announcements had been good enough to make up for this.

The job of holiday relief announcer was a handy one, for it left me freelance and able to take up contracts for other broad-casting work, apart from giving me a guaranteed five pounds a week. It also mean that It was seen regularly about the building to remind producers that my voice was still on the market. Many people in broadcasting, then as now, were neglected because they were simply forgotten; and it has been known for a producer, after scratching his head over a problem part, to bump into someone he remembered from twenty programmes back and say: 'Ah, I've got just the part for you!'

Very soon I was taken on as a permanent announcer which gave me a secure feeling, although it was certainly hard work. When I announced the early *Lift Up Your Hearts* programme, it entailed starting at seven o'clock in the morning and working right through until tea-time.

During the early announcing days a little girl wrote to the *Radio Times* to say she imagined that we all sat at a small table drinking wine! This was not so fantastic as it seemed, for in London the news readers still wore their dress suits for the evening bulletins. While we avoided this in the north, I was still able to claim the half-crown dress allowance. The hierarchy paid up reluctantly because it was a ruling in black and white that we were entitled to this half-crown, even though we never wore boiled shirts.

One day, however, when Lord Derby was giving a broadcast talk from the Manchester Studios, it was tactfully suggested that I might dress appropriately for the occasion. I carried my rigout in a suitcase to Piccadilly and changed in the announcers' office. When I was introduced to Lord Derby, his big, round face wrinkled into a smile as he exclaimed: 'Pickles, I believe you've put your dress suit on for my benefit.'

'Oh, no sir, not at all', I replied hastily, almost trying to give him the impression I wore it all day long, like a waiter.

After the broadcast, I hurried back to the office and changed again into my lounge suit. About half an hour later, fully believing that Lord Derby had left for home, I was walking along one of the corridors when suddenly I saw him, straight ahead and coming towards me. As he met me, he tugged at my sleeve and said: 'There you are, Pickles, I knew very well you had put that dress suit on for my benefit.'

A month or two afterwards, Lord Derby was to make another broadcast. He was suffering from acute rheumatism and was not fit to travel to Manchester, so the BBC took a suite at the Adelphi Hotel, Liverpool, and converted it into a studio. I was detailed to go over there to announce the programme. When I reached the hotel, I was astonished to find that the manager, thrilled at the prospect of a visit from such a great figure as Lord Derby, had lined up all his waiters, page boys and porters to form a guard of honour. There they were, in two straight files, all the way from the door to the lift. I stood at the head of this human avenue. As the Rolls-Royce drew up and Lord Derby hobbled out on two sticks, a hush descended on the hotel. There was not a sound until, as he looked up and saw me standing there, Lord Derby called out in a voice that echoed right through the building: 'Ah Pickles! Thank God you haven't put your dress suit on.'

After the broadcast, Lord Derby turned to me, smiled and sat back in relaxation.

'You come from the north, don't you?' he asked.

'I come from Yorkshire', I answered, proudly.

For a second he paused. Then he gazed straight at me and growled: 'I have a lot of my animals up in Yorkshire.'

Not all prominent people were as confident as Lord Derby before a microphone, and one of our functions as announcers was to do all we could to make speakers feel easy and help them over the various stages of 'mike-fright'. The soothing manner we had to adopt was carried to excess by one announcer who, in trying to console a member of the government, said in an encouraging tone: 'I shouldn't worry, sir, if I were you. I don't think anybody will be listening.'

There was a lighter side to Broadcasting House, and with

the whole north regional station setting a fairly high standard of performance, I found my job most congenial. I remained confused, however, as to my role inside the Corporation, not so much a feeling of unease about my actual prospects and acceptability, but more a questioning of the part played by the performers and the producers in relation to the administrators. I must confess that it is a feeling which has persisted to this day.

Time and again I have been struck by the weirdness of the workings of the Corporation, but the most baffling and discouraging fact has always been to see how remote executives were from the working broadcasters. As I came to know the Corporation better, I was more and more convinced that if broadcasting stopped for a week, the executives would not notice it and would probably think things were going a little smoother.

There is one BBC story about an executive who was leaving Broadcasting House when he was hailed by a friend who asked: 'How are things with you, old man?'

The executive stifled a yawn. 'Tired out, old boy. Fact of the matter is, there's too much darned broadcasting goes on here.'

At first I felt very removed from the top brass hierarchy in Manchester—a hierarchy whose physical anonymity left one wondering if there was not after all something behind the outward work of the BBC which was unknown to either broadcasters or listeners. Later, as my responsibilities at the Manchester studios grew, I became ranked among the senior staff of the Corporation which carried the privilege of admission to that holy of holies, the board room, for tea. It was in that rather chilling, but far from lavishly furnished room, that I met the top brass who till then had been only names to me. Apart from one or two notable exceptions they were a dull lot, so much so that I often felt that the 'bored' room would have been a more appropriate name.

The two proud mothers, Mrs Myerscough (left) and Mrs Pickles, look on as John Snagge, the inimitable voice of the BBC, proposes the toast to Wilfred and Mabel at a party to celebrate their Silver Wedding anniversary, 20 September 1955 (*Syndication International*)

A famous variety line-up from the 'fifties at the Savoy for the Pickles' 25th anniversary party: left to right, Eric Robinson, Ben Lyon, Arthur Askey between Mabel and Wilfred, Liz Welch, Turner Layton and Bebe Daniels (*Syndication International*)

Forty years on: Wilfred and Mabel drink to many more years of happy married life in September 1970 (*Sunday Express*)

Visiting the hospital ward named after them as a permanent reminder of the £100,000 which Wilfred and Mabel helped to raise for the Marie Curie Foundation (*Russell Preece*)

Typical of the BBC's resistance to change was on that fateful morning of 3 September 1939 when war was declared. Admittedly there was still an element of surprise for most people and we all continued doing our jobs as if nothing had happened. Then we learned that broadcasting from the regions was to cease, although I was still kept on as announcer without any programmes to announce! The BBC went to war gradually. New instructions would be issued and cancelled within a few hours. Small wonder then that all sorts of rumours abounded, not to mention ironical stories like the one about the two new pigeons bought by the Corporation. It was supposedly decided that it would speed things up if two Lancashire pigeons were employed to carry the more important messages. One of these birds was flying along steadily, taking its time, when the second pigeon came up behind him and said: 'Hey, Bill, what are yer messin' about for. Come on, hurry up.'

'Don't interfere with me', said the first pigeon, 'You don't seem to realise I've got a very important instruction here.'

'Aye,' said the other, 'that's what I'm telling thee to hurry up for. I've got the cancellation here.'

Even in wartime the broadcasting machine was bound so tightly with red tape that we had the ridiculous situation in which I was denied a pass to enter the building on the grounds that I was only a temporary announcer. Only permanent officials were given the permits which were so essential to get past the commissionaires. Although I was known to them by now, we had, day after day, the wearisome procedure of uniformed commissionaires having to telephone the defence officer on duty in the building to inform him that I was at the front door.

It occurred to me that, if the occasion arose when I had only minutes to spare to get to the microphone, the time lots at the front door unravelling the red tape might prove disastrous. Eventually, after a great deal of pleading and reasoning and a few plain words, I got my pass.

Being a temporary announcer had another drawback; I was not entitled to a gas mask. Members of the permanent staff were issued with service-type respirators, but I, as a temporary, did not qualify to be saved. And although I was getting used to absurdities, I rather smarted under this one!

Eventually, of course, the wheels rolled and I became eligible for a gas mask when I was made a member of the BBC's permanent staff, an unsurprising move really as I was then the senior northern announcer although still freelance. As usual I had to prove myself before being accepted by the Corporation proper, and this time at the holy of holies in London. Entering Broadcasting House in Portland Place for the first time was as terrifying an experience as my initial audition had been in Manchester, and I was rather overawed by the difference in scale between this part of the BBC and that which I had grown used to in the provinces. Everything was bigger, distressingly impersonal—and cold. I didn't like it, and felt an urge to get back to Manchester on the first train out of Euston. I was ushered into a neat and highly polished office to find myself face to face with my interviewer who asked a number of irritating questions which I considered irrelevant.

To his question: 'Where were you educated?' I lied unblinkingly. I was certain that if I had explained that I was a half-timer the day would have been a sorry one for me. Then I was asked about my religion and I wondered as In aswered what on earth that had to do with broadcasting. Finally, I must have been judged OK as I was appointed at a salary of £480 a year, a lot of money then. 'But I must warn you that if you take part in any other programmes, you will have to do them for nothing', the interviewer added, and I thought despairingly of all the work I had been doing under contract, apart from announcing. Even worse was to come, as, apparently, if I did any jobs outside the BBC for which I was paid I would have to declare such earnings to the Corporation. They were empowered to claim this money.

It was this rather parsimonious attitude to cash which I believe was responsible for the BBC losing a lot of its best men. Just such a person was Robert Reid who was seconded to the northern news editor's desk during wartime from the old *News Chronicle*. I liked him from the moment we met. He was a highly trained newspaperman who really knew his job. What's more, he hailed from Bradford, so we both spoke the same language. Sadly, he too was lured back to Fleet Street after the war.

Bob had a wonderful philosophy of life that never failed to impress me. I shall always remember the day France collapsed, for it was then that he summed up the spirit of the British people in their 'finest hour' in one of the richest remarks I have ever heard. The BBC staff were going about the studios with long faces after hearing the bad news and some of the women were in tears. Then Bob's stocky, plump figure bounced into the canteen and with a smile all over his rosy face he slapped me vigorously on the shoulder. 'Well,' he said, 'we're in t'final!'

It was this type of humour which enlivened those dark and frequently monotonous days of wartime. Then came the biggest bombshell of my broadcasting career. John Snagge telephoned from London one day to say, 'The BBC think it would be a good idea if you joined the news-reading team here.'

4 HERE IS THE NEWS

Looking back, it is difficult to credit the fuss made over the announcement of my début as a newsreader. Things moved quickly after that conversation with John Snagge and I suddenly found myself pitched into the limelight. Overnight I had apparently become the central figure in a heated national controversy. For the British people, even in the blackest days of a war that seemed to be running against them, found time to turn aside from it all to argue the rights and wrongs of the news bulletins being read in a North-Country accent. The BBC's standard English had become a firmly rooted national institution, like cricket and the pub, and Hitler or no Hitler, it meant something when there was a threat of a departure from the habit.

A press conference was called. The assembled reporters fired question after question and I had to read a newspaper story in the way I was likely to read the news from London. What impressed them most of all, naturally, was the fact that I used the short 'a', and the next morning they came out with stories with such headlines as 'Lahst a Thing of the Pahst' and 'Wilfred Pickles to stick to His Accent'.

My accent was described as 'unmistakable but not pronounced' and one journalist summed it up thus:

A devotee of the short 'a' as one hears it anywhere from Burmantofts to Irlam o' th' Heights, Wilfred firmly abjures 'larst, parst, carst' and all other usages which (to quote

Councillor Parker in Mr Priestley's play) smack of Southern 'lah-di-dah'. He has, so I gather, an especial quarrel with 'barthrum'. To a Northerner, as Wilfred reasonably points out, a 'barth' doesn't sound the least bit wet, while 'rum' is something to drink, but something to sit down in.

I was still to learn the real reason for the call to London, but picked up a little more in Portland Place when talking things over with John Snagge. For several years I had been in fairly close touch with him through memos and telephone calls and had found him easy to work with. If ever a man has lived up to the impression created by the sound of his voice it must be John Snagge, his manner was every bit as soothing as his words.

What was behind it all, I wondered. After all, the news was being read so well that I couldn't see how it could be improved. There was an excellent standard of reading set by that handful of men who had already become household names throughout Britain and the free world—Frank Phillips, Joseph McLeod, Alvar Lidell, Alan Howland and Bruce Belfrage, not forgetting the brilliant Stuart Hibberd.

John explained quite bluntly that it was not his idea. 'It's the Minister of Information, Brendan Bracken', he went on. 'He suggests a change of voice as listeners are getting a little tired of the so-called Oxford accent, and also as a security measure because your accent might not be so easily copied by the Germans.' I was rather surprised to hear of the high-level origin of the idea to give me a try-out, but more concerned that I was indeed to be given a free hand.

'If I'm going to be criticised or made to modify my style I can see myself drifting and becoming a carbon copy of the voices you've already got, and the whole experiment will fall to the ground', I said. And I also warned that my homely style was bound to creep in, because I was first and foremost an actor. I had always felt that news reading should

57

not be an impersonal affair and I knew that in reading I would fall into the habit of expressing my own feelings in my voice. Without any hesitation John Snagge replied, 'Go ahead and do as you like.'

Excitement rose as the big day approached. The press did not leave me alone and my name was appearing daily in all the national newspapers; there were jokes about 'this man from Yorkshire', and cartoonists depicted me with shirt sleeves rolled up and wearing a muffler and a cloth cap. The story was going the rounds about the conductor who, as his bus drew up at the nearest stop to the BBC, called out in a high-pitched Cockney voice: 'Broadcasting 'ouse. All alight for Wilfred Pickles!' One writer asked in print if I would say, 'Here is the news and ee bah gum this is Wilfred Pickles reading it.' There were clearly two rival factions on the issue and the constant references to me were scaring. I felt notorious and I was convinced about what was at stake.

On the day I was to be on duty at half-past four to read the six o'clock news, Mabel brought the morning papers to our hotel room. Again they carried stories about my début, and across the middle page of one were splashed the words: 'Wilfred Pickles Enters the Ring Tonight!'

I had the drill clear in my mind. After arrival at half-past four there was a visit to the news room where the bulletin was being prepared by sub-editors who passed on their 'copy' to the news editor. He in turn checked it, deleted a sentence or two and altered a few phrases. In this room, which buzzed with activity and where half a dozen typewriters continually clattered out messages for the millions, there was a long script-strewn table with a chair in the centre for the news reader and a place slightly to the right for the news editor. At the other tables sat the preoccupied, serious-faced men in shirt sleeves, who handled the news and specialised in a particular branch of the war: Russia, Middle East, home bombing or European resistance. They dictated their reports, a procedure which at least ensured that the news could be spoken.

To the left of the news reader there always sat a lady who was a living encyclopaedia on pronunciation. She advised the news readers about the way they should put over the strange foreign names of both individuals and places which so often cropped up in bulletins—particularly now that Russia was in the war. She was a godsend to the announcers. As my knowledge of languages was so scanty, I realised that I would need her assistance pretty regularly. I had noticed that the news reader initialled each page as it was passed to him by the news editor as proof that he had seen it, and that at five minutes to six he would be handed the bulletin as it stood at that moment. This up-to-the-minute technique rather staggered me, especially when I heard the news editor telling another news reader to go on with what he had. 'We'll bring the rest down later', he said.

The studio was a cramped, airless, basement room equipped with a desk, high stools like those against a bar, and two bunks for the Home Guards who stayed on all night. Straight in front of the announcer's position was a window which might have been a car windscreen and which gave a view over part of a control room where engineers turned knobs and watched meters and lights in alleys of robot-like contraptions. With consideration, somebody had supplied a blind which could be pulled down by the announcer to shut out the engineers.

On the day, I entered the studio and as I perched myself on the stool and pulled down the blind, I heard through the headphones that were lying on the desk the pips which signalled the six o'clock news. 'Here it is!' I thought. The red light flashed in and out quickly. I pressed the button which told the engineers I was ready. The red light came on and remained steady. And I was on the air with: 'This is the BBC Home and Forces Programme. Here is the news and this is Wilfred Pickles reading it.'

The bulletin was a long one and lasted about twenty minutes. Soon I was perspiring and, by the time I had finished, my face and hands were saturated, partly through nervousness and partly due to the atmosphere of the warm, enclosed studio. I drew a deep breath of great relief and Franklin Engelmann took over. As there were a few minutes before the next part of the programme, he had to put on a gramophone record and I was astonished to hear him announce: 'After what we have just heard, I think this would be a most appropriate piece of music.' And he put on 'On Ilkla Moor Baht 'At'.

Now that the first trial—and the biggest—was over, I felt quite light-hearted. Joseph Mcleod was telling me he liked the way I had read the bulletin when the phone rang. It was Mabel. I could visualise her with her eyes shining and her cheeks flushed. 'It was marvellous,' she said, 'but I'm furious!' I asked her what was wrong and she explained what had happened in the hotel as she had sat tugging nervously at a handkerchief while listening to my bulletin.

There were a number of people in the lounge when the set was switched on just before six o'clock. After I had read half the bulletin, a woman suddenly stood up and broke into the stillness by going round saying, 'Can't we switch this dreadful man off? Do you mind?' Each person acquiesed until she reached Mabel who naturally said: 'No, don't. I rather want to hear it.' So whether they liked it or not the news was left on until the very end.

In a corner of the room was a woman who, it turned out, was a Russian doctor. She must have been studying Mabel's expression, and had certainly noted the twisting handkerchief. Moving across to Mabel she said in broken English: 'Do you know this man who is reading the news?'

Rather defiantly, Mabel replied: 'Yes, as a matter of fact he's my husband.'

And the Russian doctor clapped her hands in ecstasy,

60

exclaiming: 'I knew! I knew by the sparkle in your eye!'

While I talked with Mabel, the national newspapers were lined up on the switchboard for my reactions, and this story proved the highspot for nearly all of them. Another caller was an old lady who remarked frankly and in a most endearing voice: 'I don't like you, Mr Pickles. You sound exactly like Lord Haw-Haw!'

Later, when reading the midnight news, I remembered John Snagge's words, 'Do as you like', so I rounded off the bulletin by bidding the listeners: 'Good night everybody—and to all northerners wherever you may be, good neet!' This, it was later discovered, came as an especial pleasure and a link with home to the North-Country lads serving in foreign parts, whether they were stationed in the Middle East or the south of England. I was ready for a rap from the BBC, but none came, and the first official reference to it was not made until two or three weeks afterwards when Snagge said to me: 'We rather like your good neet!'

After this came my first experience of a big fan mail. People wrote from all over Britain, from factories and air stations, London clubs and village pubs, from big houses with names and tiny cottages with numbers. But what was clear from the letters was that the people from Leeds and Manchester, and all points north, south, east and west of those cities where the short 'a' was part of the dialect, found my voice brought them a comforting feeling that the old familiar places and faces were still there. Yet while the praise came to me, the abuse poured into the postal section of the BBC. With a party political truce in force for the duration of the war it seemed that the public were ready to snatch at any topic with a controversial angle and, their appetites whetted by the popular press, they seized on this issue.

An interesting fact that emerged from my advent as a news reader was that while letters of complaint had poured into the BBC, the results of a door-to-door listener-research canvas indicated quite definitely that my reading was very popular. One surprising revelation that arose out of the researchers' quest was that my news reading was more popular in the south than in the north of England.

While I have the greatest respect for the many achievements of the BBC, I believe that for years they were guilty of the offence of trying to teach Great Britain to talk standard English. How terrible it is to think that we may some day lose the soft Devonshire accent, or the bluff Scots brogue, or the flatness and forthrightness of the North-Countryman's speech. May it be forbidden that we all should ever speak 'Oxford English', for our rich contrast of voices is a vocal tapestry of great beauty and incalculable value, handed down to us by our forefathers. Our dialects are reminders of the permanence of things in these islands of ours, where people talk differently in places only five miles apart, a phenomenon that has its roots in the times when it took many days to ride from London to York by stagecoach. Some countries have grown up at seventy miles an hour in an age of TV and telephones—but not ours, thank goodness.

I should be very happy if I could know now that when I die a Yorkshireman will say: 'He were a champion fella' and a Lancashire man will comment: 'He wor a gradely mon'. That would be praise indeed. The North-Country dialects are for ever being ridiculed, but if they go, much of our character goes too. The view that if a man speaks in a North-Country accent he must necessarily wear a cloth cap and keep a whippet under the table should be squashed; we must see to it that we don't speak in one language.

Here we are in a country flowing with folk songs, compositions that belong essentially to the people and which are sung by working men and women instead of professional singers. But who does anything about preserving them? Unless someone, and the broadcasters in particular, gets out and about to record such songs pretty soon they are going to die with this generation just as the Lancashire poetry has died.

In an age of increasing equality, when a regional accent is no longer a stumbling block in many fields, some people may think that I still take this question of speech rather too seriously. Well, the Beatles may have made 'Scouse' fashionable for a period in the sixties, and the Geordie twang is experiencing a revival in these days of economic gloom when we look back at the effect of the thirties' depression on such places as Tyneside, but I have a sneaking feeling that whilst it's all right for pop stars and playwrights to speak in their native tones, aspiring leaders of men must take more care. Why else is it that the current Conservative leadership speaks in such flat, uninspiring tones with such careful vowel sounds and so little feeling?

And the broadcasting companies, with anchor men like arts pundit Melvyn Bragg from Cumberland, now with commercial television, and the BBC's Manchester-based Brian Redhead tackling current affairs, would be quick to say that they give due national prominence to people who are good at their jobs whatever their accent. Isn't it odd then that we hear so few members of our now long-established immigrant communities as announcers and interviewers.

Equally, although I don't wish to be involved in any arguments about women's lib, while on the subject of broadcast speech, I was astonished to read the other day that the admirable Angela Rippon is now being castigated by some of her male colleagues for her apparently idiosyncratic way of pronouncing certain proper names. Well, well, and yet she's still chosen as Newscaster of the Year. It's not just cricket is it, chaps? To me, Ms Rippon manages to achieve that truly impersonal approach which I always found so foreign to my nature. Still, I wish she'd stick to the news reading and forget about the high kicks. . . .

Newscasters appearing in light entertainment shows, the

monarchy willingly playing 'starring' roles in suitable television programmes, film violence on the increase and nudity now seen on our screens as much as in our homes—yes the BBC has come a long way since Lord Reith's days. All true Corporation men recall with delight the story of how John Snagge once caught one of the radio news readers making love to a secretary in a BBC studio of all places. Being told of this from another source, Lord Reith was all for dismissing the unlucky character on the spot. Summoning Snagge to his office, the Director General gave his orders, but Snagge dug his heels in, saying 'No. He is one of my best newsreaders'. There was a pause, during which Reith's Scots Presbyterian background could be heard battling with his professional self. 'Very well,' he finally uttered, 'he shall stay, but never again must he read the *Epilogue.*'

5 MAKING 'EM LAUGH—
AND CRY

I have never spoken a truer word than when I told John Snagge that I was an actor first and foremost. And, whilst my days as a national newscaster were productive, I always felt constrained at having to push my natural ebullience into the background. Equally, living in a London hotel room was no substitute for family life, and it was with a sigh of relief that we returned home to Manchester at the end of my news-reading stint. Now, more than ever, I was anxious to be my real self, to communicate with people on a one-to-one basis if possible rather than representing the voice of authority.

During the stay in London I had become known in the studios for my North-Country stories, and I was developing a humorous streak which had begun in early variety shows such as *Two's a Crowd*, with Jack Train, and *Kingpins of Comedy*, where I interviewed such great comics as Arthur Askey, Ted Ray, Tommy Handley and Georgie Wood. Having made a stir as a news reader, I decided that the time was ripe, while my name was fairly fresh in the public mind, to approach John Sharman, the veteran producer of *Music Hall*, about a chance in his show. I telephoned him and pointed out that I had a fund of Lancashire and Yorkshire tales which I had collected since boyhood.

John promised me a spot, and soon I was on my way to Bangor (the BBC's secret hideout which nearly everybody knew about) to take part in *Music Hall*. I was most impressed with this friendly town, and indeed whenever I have visited

Wales I have invariably found an honest welcome and a genuine warm-heartedness among the people. I heard a lot of good stories from these sturdy, lively folks, most of whom have grown up in conditions which were far from being the most likely to stimulate a sense of humour. One that amused me tremendously was about a certain Dai Jones who had a broody hen. With the hen under his arm he called at the local general store kept by Mrs Williams. 'What do you want, Dai?' she asked, to which Dai replied: 'Have you any nice new laid eggs?'

'No,' she replied, 'but I have some lovely tomatoes.'

'Damn,' said Dai, 'They're no use to me; it's a broody hen I've got here, not a broody greenhouse.'

Nobody could have improved on *Music Hall*. It was under regular criticism for as long as I can remember, but the critics offered no constructive suggestions as to how it might be improved. There were six artistes on the bill that day and John made a most generous gesture by placing me fifth in order of appearance. Announced as 'the man who has recently read the news', I got a really warming reception from the audience and my stories, it seemed, went down well with the listeners.

How grateful I was then that I had not forsaken my origins. Use of the genuine expression 'Ee doctor, I've come on a right cheeky errand' when describing someone wishing to discuss an intimate physical complaint would set exactly the right tone for a story, however innocent the punchline turned out to be. And use of real background material always helped. For instance, the desire of the efficient northern grandmother always to be on hand at a birth, gave substance to the delightful story of the little boy who went to school rather depressed that his position in the household had been ousted by the birth of a brother. In an effort to cheer him up the young teacher said 'You are lucky, Johnny. I wish I could have a baby too.'

'Well', replied the young man of the world. 'It's very simple. All you do is have a bath, put on a clean nightie and send for my granny'!

The newspaper still regarded me as a topical personality and out came the stories. One writer commented: 'If this is Mr Pickles as a comedian let's have more of him.'

Practically every agent in London wrote suggesting that if I could continue to turn out material like that I had used in my spot on *Music Hall*, there was a chance for me on the variety stage. We selected Julius Darewski to handle my affairs and he suggested first a season at the Blackpool Opera House with George Black, then a tour of the music halls, and at Christmas a pantomime.

Mabel, however, was still cautious. 'Who is going to look after Wilfred's interests while he is in these shows, and what's going to happen afterwards?' she asked.

'Afterwards!' Julius drummed the edge of his desk with his fingertips. 'Mrs Pickles,' he said, 'you don't realise you have got a diamond here.'

'I know I have,' Mabel shot back. 'But I want to make sure the diamond is in its right setting!'

Julius grinned and I roared with laughter at Mabel's directness, and the Chinese proverb flashed through my mind: 'The road to success is crowded with women pushing their husbands along'.

After working out a month's notice with the BBC and snatching one quiet weekend at home, we set out again, this time for Cambridge and the aerodromes and Army camps that had mushroomed round the ancient town. With me at the top of the ENSA bill for the tour was that attractive, pleasant, and, we were soon to discover, wholly sincere personality—Vera Lynn. In her sincerity she reminded me of another artiste I had known and admired for years, Donald Peers. Donald had told me of his humble origin and his early struggles, and it was clear early on that one day he would be the Bing Crosby of Great Britain. Like Donald, Vera sang popular songs with such feeling that the fighting men scattered all over the world took her to their hearts. Her records of tunes like 'I'll Be Seeing You' and 'Coming Home' were played until the tracks wore out. To the soldier in the steaming jungle swamp and the sentries in the outposts of the world she was the girl back home. She represented all that was fresh and delightful, all that they were fighting for. Seeing her again on the *This Is Your Life* programme in honour of Lord Louis Mountbatten, I was reminded how much she still stands for all that is worthwhile in the English way of life.

How clearly some of our wartime humour stands out in retrospect. It was part of our armour; it rattled our enemies and took away the strain. During the battle of Britain, a story was told in a Manchester club about the Spitfire pilot who, as he drifted down on the end of a parachute, saw a woman coming up towards him. 'Have you seen my Spitfire going down?' he yelled. And back came the reply: 'No, I haven't, young man. Have you seen my gas cooker going up?' Who in the world can say why that is funny?

It is even harder to take Robb Wilton's fun to pieces for scientific analysis. Yet the inimitable Robb had the nation roaring with laughter during those years of desperate anxiety and peril. Who will ever forget the cautiously protesting henpecked voice coming out of the loudspeaker with those plaintive and memorable words that sum up an unforgettable milestone in the lives of most of us: 'The wife said to me— "What're you doin' to help?" And I said: "Doing? I'm guarding England." She said: "You are?" I said: "Well, there's me . . . and Fred Ingham . . . and Jack Smith!" '

Mabel has often reminded me of the time when Robb and I were introduced from the same platform by a mayor. Portentously, and with the air of one who knows, he glanced in turn at Robb and myself and then announced us as 'two

The *Have a Go* team in the Millwall Docks canteen at the height of the show's success in 1950. With Wilfred and a contestant are Mabel (far left) at the table with the gong, standing, Barney Colehan, producer and, seated at the piano, Violet Carson (*Radio Times Hulton Picture Library*)

Have a Go has a fling in the Highlands (*Syndication International*)

Wilfred, taking a break from playing Buttons in the 1951 record-breaking run of *Cinderella* in Leeds, with that best of companions, writer J.B. Priestley

Pickles the radio actor, seen here with Megs Jenkins rehearsing for Joseph Colton's comedy, *The Gay Dog*, broadcast in the Saturday-Night Theatre series (*BBC*)

of the most famous names in Britain—household words—names every child in the street knows!' And he concluded: 'On my left, ladies and gentlemen, is Wilfred Wilton and on my right the one and only Robb Pickles!'

Robb and I glanced across at each other and burst out laughing with the rest of the people there. Then, very astutely and with the sharpness of the born humorist, Robb piped up with: 'As the Town Clerk has just told you—' The rest was drowned in a renewed outburst of laughter as His Worship protested: 'Nay, nay, lad—I'm t'Mayor!'

Our month with the troops at an end, we found ourselves on the move again, this time heading for Blackpool. Looking at the vast array of luggage—wardrobe trunks, personal suitcases and bags, I reflected on those days so many years ago when my mother packed for a week's holiday at the same resort. What would she have thought if, like Mabel, she had had to pack for eighteen weeks. It was almost like emigrating!

At the theatre a bright poster loudly proclaimed:

GEORGE BLACK'S SUMMER SHOW
We're All In It
Wilfred Pickles
Rawicz and Landauer
Jewell and Warriss
Elisabeth Welch
Steffani's Silver Songsters; Tommy Jover;
Nena and Raff; Charles Warren and Jean; Phyllis Hunter;
and the Dagenham Girl Pipers

Seeing this enormous billing made me wonder whether I could live up to the reputation that my performance in John Sharman's *Music Hall* had given me, whether I would get the same laughs, the same welcome. I was still wondering, but more anxiously, as I stood in the wings on the opening night and heard the orchestra and the tumult of clapping from the three thousand people in the theatre.

It was a typical first night. The chorus sang the number by which I was introduced. In the middle of their vocal all the girls on the stage leaned forward urgently with their hands cupped against their ears in an attitude of listening. The music stopped suddenly to give me my cue to say through a microphone offstage: 'This is the BBC Home and Forces Programme. Here is the news and by gum this is Wilfred Pickles reading it.'

What a build-up! But at the crucial moment the microphone went dead. The audience was left bewildered as to what the pause and the ear-cupping attitude of the girls might represent and I made my entrance to a stony silence, my impressive introduction lost. After all, why should these people know me? But as soon as I opened my mouth and said 'Ow do, 'ow are yer?' the audience rose and gave me a terrific ovation.

Headlines followed: 'Pickles Makes Stage Hit', said the *Sunday Chronicle* the following morning, while an evening paper came out with: 'This is Real Black Magic', and went on to say: 'Few guessed what an ordeal it was. But the Northerner who took languid out of language on the air had made thousands more friends when the curtain fell.'

The whole show was a success. It brought thousands into the theatre and I believe I am right in saying that the record of packed houses it established still stands today. Not that success was allowed to go to my head. How well I remember getting tickets for a friend to a show in which I starred at the old Sheffield Empire where one of the supporting acts was Olsen and his sealion. After the performance I waited for his reactions. As none came I prompted him gently with 'Well, what did you think?'

Truthful as ever he replied, 'That sealion wor bloody marvellous'!

From Blackpool we started a tour of the music halls that was to carry us all over the country and give us a rare glimpse of the way variety artistes live and work—but mostly work! Then we went to Liverpool for my pantomime engagement as Pickles the Page in Tom Arnold's *The Sleeping Beauty*. The pantomime meant more hard work and with two performances every day, Mabel and I only breathed fresh air when we walked from the Adelphi Hotel through Lime Street Station to the Empire Theatre. I believe it was my dresser who told us: 'You know, the work's harder in panto than in any other part of show business—and especially for the comedian.'

And yet I remained fascinated by the opportunity of pantomime and signed a two-season contract to play Buttons in *Cinderella* at the Alhambra, Bradford, and the Theatre Royal, Leeds, mainly because it was a sympathetic part that allowed a bit of acting and also because the character was a favourite among children who, I felt, might remember me when they were grown older as the first Buttons they ever saw.

Working with the king of pantomime, the kindly, mild and self-effacing but keen-eyed Francis Laidler, was an even more exacting business than my pantomime baptism had been. From the moment the company set foot on the stage for the first rehearsal Mr Laidler lived pantomime. He left nothing to chance, and when he signed on four beautiful white ponies to draw Cinderella to the ball in the glittering stagecoach, he remarked that one of them looked rather fat.

'Aye, she's going to foal—but it won't happen until after the pantomime', said their owner reassuringly.

'All right', said Laidler. But the same morning he was on the telephone to his stage manager. 'We'll design the coach so that it can be pulled by three ponies—just in case', he said, refusing to be dependent on Dame Nature.

As Cinderella was drawn off the stage with the fairy giving her directions to leave the ball 'ere the clock strikes twelve', my part as the forlorn figure of Buttons, left all alone again, was to run after the luxurious, dazzling coach, holding a faded bunch of flowers.

Although the ponies were extraordinarily well behaved and there had been no accidents, I had always at the back of my mind the fear that something might happen one night, and I arranged to have a stagehand waiting with a small shovel and brush. Performance after performance without incident for weeks: then came the emergency. It was certainly not in keeping with the romantic story of *Cinderella*, and the audience seemed slightly embarrassed, so I seized the shovel and brush and dashed on to sweep up the gardeners' fertiliser. My efforts relieved the tension and produced such a roar that immediately I left the stage I sent for Fred the property man and asked him if we could have some artificial manure. He suggested it could be made out of canvas and that each of the four chorus girls who led on the ponies should conceal it in their hands and drop it as the ponies started to move off. It was a bright idea for which I did not get Mr Laidler's consent, and just before I followed the coach with my shovel and brush I noticed he was sitting in his usual place in the stalls with his notebook on his knees, a notebook he always carried to jot down anything of which he disapproved in the production.

As the coach moved slowly and gracefully off the stage I watched for the falling canvas. The pieces were dropped and I rushed forward. But they bounced! Like rubber balls they bobbed up and down towards the footlights with me careering after them. There was not a sound from the audience, not a movement. I wanted somebody to let the curtain fall quickly. No one seemed to have the slighest idea what I was supposed to be doing, and the look one of those ponies gave me afterwards I could never describe.

I had hardly got into my dressing-room when there was a gentle tap on the door. 'It's all right, Mr Laidler', I called, knowing who it must be. 'It's out—from now!'

74

Well, pantomime was certainly an experience, but, although I have always enjoyed comedy hugely, I think that some of my most rewarding moments have been on the 'legitimate' stage, achieving those teenage ambitions nurtured so keenly in Halifax and Southport before earning a living became of prime importance, sweeping aside my thoughts of tragic heroes and romantic leads.

Perhaps my happiest acting role came when my agent rang to say that the great actor Robert Donat was leaving *The Cure For Love*, Walter Greenwood's Lancashire comedy which was running at the Westminster Theatre. Was I interested in taking over the part? This was indeed something I really wanted to do. Straight acting. Was I interested!

I was overwhelmed at the prospect of once again playing a leading part in a straight play after all these years and as I went to the theatre for an interview with the producer, I wondered what sort of reception I would get from that giant of the theatrical world, H. K. Ayliff, whose name I had known so long.

As I arrived at the theatre much too early for my appointment, I became increasingly apprehensive about my capacity to play the part, until finally I worked myself into such a state of uncertainty that I found I was half hoping that Ayliff would turn me down. Even if he accepted me, I had an excuse: 'Trouble with me is that I'm not big enough to play the soldier. Donat is fairly tall and would not look out of place as a sergeant. I wouldn't be right, especially as the fellow in the play is something of a boxer.'

It came almost as a shock when I realised I had actually spoken these words to Ayliff. He waved an arm. 'Ridiculous! We'll make you a lightweight, a featherweight—or whatever they call them in that dreadful business!'

Ayliff stressed that I would have to learn and rehearse the part and be on the stage as Sergeant Hardacre in ten days. As I had grown so accustomed to radio scripts and to the individualistic methods of variety shows, I knew I would not find it easy to learn the part. We arranged that I should start rehearsals at ten o'clock the following morning.

Throughout that afternoon and evening, breaking off only to eat, we read and re-read the script, Mabel taking every part except that of Sergeant Hardacre. Night after night we went through the play so that by the end of the week Mabel had lost her voice completely. I was already learning that the task of succeeding to the part was no less unenviable than I had imagined just before I met Ayliff. After all, I was leaping into the midst of a polished West End company who had been together for almost four months. They were absolute masters of their parts and knew the play backwards.

Then came yet another first night, and this time one especially important for me. I stood in the wings with a kitbag over one shoulder and rifle slung over the other wondering if I really looked like a homecoming sergeant. As the cue line approached I thought: 'This is it'; but my anxiety had given way to a confidence that had been inspired chiefly by the thoroughness of Ayliff's rehearsals. I felt comfortable on the stage, happy in the part, and never forgot a word. The audience called for a curtain speech. Mabel was overjoyed and Ayliff came round to the dressing-room and said: 'Never alter it. Just keep it as it is.'

What a success that show was, running for five more months in the West End before going on to a two-year provincial tour. BBC commitments forced me to refuse the part at the start of the tour, although I was eventually able to rejoin the cast later. How I loved those tours, despite the constant moving on and often cramped surroundings. However, I've always been a great one for theatrical digs, managing to make myself at home wherever I stay. One theatrical land-lady in particular stands out, Manchester's Mrs McKay. Now in her seventies, she still provides magnificent food and marvellous rooms. I'm sure that every actor in the profession must have stayed with her some time in his life. We were last there in 1976 when I was working as the Labour Party agent for a troubled MP, played by Tony Britten in Granada TV's *The Nearly Man*. Actors complaining of the rigours of the stage might have a shock if they played in a long-running TV series. *The Nearly Man* was a full-time job, thirteen episodes, rehearsed and recorded from ten till six during the week. At the same time I was also introducing *Stars on Sunday* for Yorkshire Television in Leeds which involved a 6 am start one day and work in the studios there before returning to Manchester to continue the serial. So comfortable digs were a real must during that period.

Good theatrical lodgings are also a godsend to impoverished actors, especially the members of the chorus, who can't afford high prices for hotel rooms, and who would gladly rub along with their fellow performers at reasonable rates rather than remaining in some sort of secluded luxury. I've always appreciated the story of the actor who had received particularly good reviews so decided to treat himself to a piece of steak accompanied by asparagus. He duly bore the food home and entrusted it to his landlady for that evening's supper. On his return, he was greeted by a succulent smell of steak and a landlady who remarked, 'Well, your steak's doing nicely, and I've put the bluebells in water.'

That may be a part of theatrical lore, but I can vouch for the lovely gaffe made by a supposed theatre buff in Oldham who, when he heard we were going to Stratford said, 'You simply must stay in the hotel where all the rooms are named after Shakespeare's plays. You know, like . . . *The Mikado*'!

Although I've had some notable successes in the theatre, I can't honestly say that it's because of my own unerring eye for a play. In fact, one of my most memorable roles was suggested by the Master himself, Noël Coward. As we were dressing together one evening at the Irene Vanburgh Theatre he suddenly said, 'You must play Willie Mossop in *Hobson's*

Choice.' That proved to be an extremely sound judgement and
the part brought much pleasure to me and packed audiences.
It also, inadvertently, gave me a near miss, that of meeting
the Queen Mother. Part of the performance called for me to
be on a hoist, a position in which I was forced to remain
while her Royal Highness received the rest of the cast!

I've also been involved in some spectacular theatrical
flops. A few years ago I turned down the part of the father in
Spring and Port Wine, the popular revival of the North-
Country family saga, which eventually ran for five years
with Alfred Marks in the starring role. Instead I accepted
the lead in *Come Laughing Home*, a new play by those excellent
modern writers Keith Waterhouse and Willis Hall. Sadly, it
only ran for two weeks. We began our out-of-town run at
Wimbledon and the play was already doomed by Golders
Green. As we came out of the theatre for the last time the
bills were still up saying 'World Première'.

Whilst few modern playwrights achieve the success of, say
an Alan Ayckbourn, with several plays running in the West
End concurrently, many write excellent TV scripts. My
greatest admiration goes to such teams as Dick Clements and
Ian La Fresnais, creators of the inimitable *Porridge* and
especially to Vince Powell and the late Harry Driver who
wrote *For Love of Ada*, a big TV comedy success for Irene
Handl and me. The touching situation of the marriage of
two old-age pensioners, widow and widower who met at the
graveside, was laced with wit, and the sparks which flew
when the couple came up against each other made for a show
which ran for six series.

As a medium, television has its own rules, and certain
situations which work well in the theatre do not work well on
the box and vice versa. I'm frequently astonished by TV
attempts to reproduce stage hits, taking out much of the
body from the language which made the play in the theatre
and replacing it by tricky camera work as well as expensively

conceived outdoor shots. A good example, to my mind, of a great play which failed to transfer successfully to the small screen was Laurence Olivier's direction of *Hindle Wakes*, the concentration on effective and 'meaningful' shots leaving little time for development of character or for giving due prominence to the play's real meaning.

But any actor's view of a play or a fellow actor's performance must be subjective as he reads his own interpretation of the lines into what the man playing the part is saying. And, of course, the public watching the drama unfold will draw their own conclusions as to character, cause and effect. It's easy to lose a sense of balance when getting too close to great plays. Perhaps the most truthful line came from the old repertory actor, when asked by an enthusiastic student of *Hamlet*, 'Was Ophelia a virgin?' 'Never in my time, laddie. No, never in my time,' came back the reply!

6   HAVING A GO

All my life I have been fascinated by people, especially the ordinary working man. Walking through London or Manchester on my way to the studios it often struck me how much the hundreds of figures surging by on the pavements recalled the paintings of that great Lancastrian artist L. S. Lowry. All those anonymous men and women. Where did they work? What were their homes like? What were their hopes, ambitions, fears?

Work done, hundreds of people would make their way home in laughing groups, with, here and there, a lone figure hurrying or disconsolately ambling, but always moving at a pace different from the rest. Most of them carried lunch boxes and the northern men nearly all wore cloth caps. Passing them, I came to pick out faces I had seen before: carefree faces, worried faces, hungry faces and well-fed ones, they were all there, although the general impression I got was of a feeling of relief that another day's work was over. My curiosity about these characters increased. I wanted to follow them home, eat with them and have a chat with them about what they wanted to do with their lives.

I wanted to break down their common anonymity. Even inside Broadcasting House I kept thinking of those folks I had passed on my way in, living in obscure side streets where the sun never got a look in and where none but the residents and the rent collectors ever called. My most frightening thought was that I should be confined to one of these streets for the rest of my days. Yet I wanted to visit these people and see how they lived and what they did with their spare time. I vowed I would try to find the answers to all my questions.

What uncovered human stories there were in those alleys and sitting rooms and kitchens! At that time, the ordinary people who made up the real-life scene were not given a look-in on the air. Yet, at the time, the BBC was presenting stage plays that were much better handled by the theatre, and snippets from films which were far, far better seen in a cinema. Could the BBC not go down Back Lane and call at number forty and get a real story? For surely there was one. I remembered there was *In Town Tonight*, but odd characters were chosen, and I thought how much more interesting and original an interview would be with the labourer next door who swung a shovel for nine hours a day than with the man who had hitch-hiked all the way from India to Newcastle. The BBC interviewed people who could only 'happen' in the newspapers! They were unreal and not part of our lives.

It was while such thoughts were uppermost in my mind that the BBC decided to revive 'Harry Hopeful', a happy-go-lucky character who wandered round the country meeting ordinary people and bringing them to the microphone in their natural environment, whether it was the country pub or the village church hall. Harry had tramped through places like the Trough of Bowland, that jewel of nature in the heart of Lancashire, and the windswept countryside between Kendal and Windermere. I was offered the main role and, as the old name could obviously no longer be used, I came up with Billy Welcome as an appropriate title for a roving interviewer.

The BBC looked on the programme as something of a morale-booster. Producer Geoffrey Bridson and I started off the series with a walk from Appleby to Richmond in Yorkshire, bringing in the spacious, enchanting Dales. There we came across the eighty-year-old cobbler, Mr Alderson, who lived in the pretty village of Gunnerside with his daughter. A couple of bombs had recently been dropped on the surrounding moorland by a tip-and-run raider. The daughter told how she was awakened by a loud bang and thought to herself: 'That's father falling out of bed! Then there was another big bang and I thought: "Nay, he can't do it twice"', she laughed. She told us also about a Mr Reynolds who had written a hymn tune called 'Gunnerside' which he sang along with her father and a farmer at their local concerts and social functions.

'I'll get them together if you like', she said eagerly. And as we waited round the log-stocked hearth of the Yorkshire cottage she went off to find them. In about ten minutes she was back; the farmer had evidently been dragged from his work for he was still in his farming clothes, collarless with dirt-caked boots and breeches. After brief introductions Mr Reynolds sat at the piano and the three men started singing that very beautiful tune. It was a scene made for television rather than radio, with the strong, leathery faces of the cobbler and the farmer and the smile of pride on the daughter's face. That hymn 'Gunnerside', was haunting. As I remembered its notes I realised more clearly than ever before just how much the love of one's own little place on the map means.

The programme was well received and was the forerunner of many more. We travelled the length and breadth of these islands in our search for new people and places. I was learning a lot about those ordinary people as we journeyed throughout the land. Although struck by the high morale of people in such hard times it was what they said spontaneously before a microphone that intrigued and excited me, and I was astounded at the popularity of the programmes. People liked to hear what the man down the street or the woman with the basket in the shopping queue thought about things.

82

On an exploratory trip into Yorkshire prior to another broadcast, I came across a farmer muck-spreading on some of his productive acres. He wore high leggings fastened with heavy leather laces that were plastered over with dried mud and he had no collar, his thick blue-striped flannel shirt being fastened at the neck by a large shining stud. I leaned over the fence and started chatting with him. Like many countrymen, when given the opportunity to talk he became really voluble. Eventually I told him I was from the BBC and asked if he would like to repeat on the air what he had just said. He gazed at me from beneath a pair of bushy eyebrows and said: 'Ah've a daughter in America an' if she 'ears 'er owd father on t'wireless she'll laugh like 'ell.'

I asked if he would object if I wrote down a few things he had said and he replied: 'There're a few more things 'n that. A few things I want to say to t'Milk Marketing Board!' I treasured such gems from the people, though I had long since ceased to be astonished at their discovery.

It was an old fisherman at Kirkcudbright who taught me that a rough face and a thick jersey often go with character of high quality. Talking in one of the early *Billy Welcome* programmes, he answered my request that he should tell me all about himself by saying quite simply:

That's a tall order, but I'll gie ye a wee keek into my life. I was born seventy-five years ago with the sound of the sea in my ears. As I grew up I looked forward to the day when I would go to sea as my father and forefathers had before me. To me the sea was something rosy and beautiful, but now, as I reach the latter years of my life, I see her darker moods of treachery and instability.

Then, with a faraway look in his eyes he recalled some of the fellows he had known:

And then there was auld Andy. Puir auld Andy some people would call him. I can see him now going down the street after digging for lugworm for bait, wi' his can on his back and his

83

white hair streaming on his shoulders, an' singin', as only he could sing: 'Ah'm a pilgrim bound for glory; Ah'm a pilgrim coming hame'. I almost said 'puir auld Andy'. Puir he was as this world knows it but if auld Andy isna in Heaven, ah dinna want to go there, for believe me there canna be any.

Then the BBC decided to turn *Billy Welcome* into a propaganda programme. It disturbed me to have to go into canteens of great industrial firms and ordnance works and work up a frenzy of patriotism, national fervour and a 'go-to-it' spirit among the overalled, grease-stained men and women. I hated the job. There were marching songs and sentimental melodies and I would interview these folks about their war jobs. There were the personal endeavour stories in which a young mother told us about her own effort. 'Looking after three children and still doing a grand job in the factory. Good lass', I would say, giving her a pat on the back. How I loathed it, and how embarrassed I felt.

For me the programme had lost its honesty and its pleasing simplicity. It was rank propaganda under a cloak of entertainment and it tormented me throughout the several months that it ran. I gradually came almost to despise Billy Welcome, who by now was not feeling anything like so hearty as he had to appear to the various munition workers.

I was more than pleased then when the programme was discontinued, although the experience had stood me in good stead for what was to follow. It was when John Salt, then programme director of the north region, telephoned to say that he had an idea we could do 'an important programme together' that I unwittingly became a part of the show which was to have the greatest influence on my life and still remains linked with my name for many people throughout the country.

John Salt developed the idea of the programme; a quiz in which money would be given away for correct answers to three or four questions. 'I want to get away from scripted programmes, to find something spontaneous', he said. 'We must get out and about, visit a different place each week . . .'

'And interview ordinary folks', I said, becoming more and more interested.

'Most certainly', John replied. And noticing my rising enthusiasm, he went on: 'We'll get down to it right away.'

This was the beginning then of *Have a Go*. In its twenty-one-year run, we covered some 400,000 miles, as far as the moon and back. Millions of people throughout the British Isles and in other parts of the world, too, made a regular date with the programme. BBC men marvelled at its success. Critics and psychologists tried to analyse its popularity. I was even told it was a passing fad. It had lived up to its advance description of being 'astonishingly simple'. We could fill Brighton's Royal Pavilion, but we could make do just as well with a little wooden hut or a canteen; the people interviewed were ordinary men and women being themselves, most of whom had never even seen a microphone.

And the things they said were equally spontaneous and unrehearsed. For example, when I interviewed an elderly beekeeper I asked him if it were true that bee stings prevented rheumatism, and he replied that this was indeed the case. Later, however, when I wondered why his wife wasn't in the audience, he revealed that she was unable to get out as 'She's a bit rheumaticky at the moment'! At a little village called Kettlesing, six miles outside Harrogate, a fellow came to the microphone who had seven sons, the eldest being thirty-five. Anxious to know what the ages of the others were I asked: 'And what do they come down to?'

Somewhat at a loss, he replied 'Oh, they come down to Harrogate, mostly.'

People revealed an engaging simplicity with which so many others could identify. Like the woman who told me that she worked in a lovely house for very rich people. 'You can tell how wealthy they are' she confided, 'they even have fruit on the sideboard when no one's poorly.'

As mentioned previously, the quiz element of the show was never over-emphasised and gradually it began to be less and less important as the people's characters and their anecdotes took over. Many listeners were incensed during the early days when I used to 'gong' contestants who couldn't answer their questions, as this seemed to take away much of the show's friendly spirit. I tended to agree with them. Who cared whether an old woman who had just told us how she reared a family of twelve could say where the Alps were? So the gong went on strike. Mabel hit it only to herald the start of each programme, and the confidence in folk's minds that they would not be gonged made them less cautious in answering questions, with the result that we got some classic replies. Once when I asked 'What is the renewal date for a dog licence?', I received the quick reply 'Seven-and-sixpence'.

Gradually my 'stock' questions such as 'What was your most embarassing moment?', 'If you weren't you, who would you like to be?', 'If you had to pass a law to benefit mankind, what would it be?' and, of course, the ever-popular one to a young man or woman 'Are ya coortin?' became the programme's hall-marks and the side of the show to which people most responded.

As *Have a Go* captured the public fancy, my fan mail leapt to between five and six hundred letters a week. It represented a very full-time job and was clearly too big a task for Mabel to cope with on top of her usual work; so we engaged two secretaries and converted the lounge of our home in Manchester, already stripped of furniture which had gone to the London flat, into an office.

Whenever I could snatch a few moments I would start to read the pile of letters myself. They came from the old and the very young, ex-Servicemen, teachers and tailors; there were notes from those who were sick and the robust ones with energy to spare; and the addresses reflected every economic

Playing the hard but honest Labour agent to Tony Britton's mixed-up MP in the television serial, *The Nearly Man* (*Granada Television*)

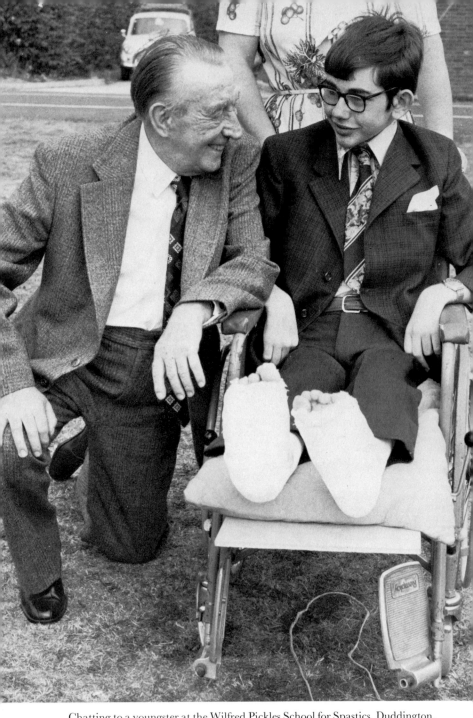

Chatting to a youngster at the Wilfred Pickles School for Spastics, Duddington, Lincs in July '76

level. Some of the writing was copperplate, some an indecipherable scrawl. Many of the letters told deeply moving stories and I present them here merely to show what effect this very human programme was having on the thoughts and actions of our listeners. Among them was this beautifully expressed one from Jeanette Linkova, living in Czechoslovakia:

> I at first hesitated to write, as I wondered if you would ever read the letter. But on second thoughts I took up my pen to say 'thank you' sincerely and heartfeltly. I listen to you and the people you introduce, with mixed feelings. Laughter comes spontaneously, yet tears are close behind. Maybe this is always so. I try to join in the songs, but always my voice breaks and no sound comes. Since I came here I have fought against homesickness. I stay because I feel my duty lies here. I married a Czech in the war; we lived in London till 1944 when a V1 hit our home and killed my husband and best friend. I came here in 1945 with my baby son to find the parents who knew nothing of their son since 1939. I found them, stayed, married my brother-in-law and now have two sons. Many people have left, but more people's happiness demands that I stay.... Although on paper I have lost my British nationality I feel a great warm glow of pride when I listen to *Have a Go*. This is the humour of the land, the ordinary everyday citizens who 'make' a country. I thank you and your partners.

One little girl of six wrote an essay at school which was sent to me by her mother: 'I like Wilfred Pickles because he is nice. If he would come to live with me I would like him to put his feet on my hot water bottle and I would give him some bacon and some tea and buy him some new clothes.' Obviously they were all the things she liked herself—and she honoured me by offering to give me a share!

A Leicester old-age pensioner sent these words:

> My wife is seventy-five years of age and after working for over sixty years, and over sixty years' social and religious work, has had two seizures and now has a useless leg, arm and badly affected speech. I would like you to see her face as your name is

F

mentioned. It lights up with eager expectation and she calls out: 'Let's have a go' before you do. It is worth more than the licence fee to see her so happy. 'Turn on the radio. You know Wilfred starts very punctual.' That has just been called out to me.

And, to be fair, there was the occasional letter of complaint.

One northerner was typically blunt: 'Young man, you're in t'wrong job. Why don't you get out of this broadcasting and get into something that suits you better. I must admit I've listened and I don't like you.'

Mabel and I worked out a reply which she typed. It read: 'I am sorry you don't like me but one day perhaps I will do something you will like. As I am broadcasting next Tuesday, I wonder if you would care to listen and let me have your reactions.'

The broadcast was made as planned; Wednesday went by, and on Thursday morning among the mail was an envelope we recognised. Eagerly I tore it open. 'Dear Wilfred', he wrote, 'Well, I listened—and I still don't like thee!'

Nor was life within the Corporation always easy. After a most moving broadcast from St George's Crypt, Leeds, a temporary haven for down-and-outs—a programme fully sanctioned by the BBC—the public responded marvellously to the plight of these misfits and showered the centre with gifts. A special mail van had to be diverted to the crypt and, in all, some £3,000 poured in plus a roomful of clothes. Apparently such a programme was thought to cut across the BBC Appeals Committee and a memo duly came ordering such broadcasts to stop. As fund-raising had never been in my mind throughout the show, I was obviously saddened by this beaurocratic lack of understanding, but was even more upset when told that *Have a Go* must cease broadcasting from hospitals, another decision which possibly had some sound factual base, although I was never given a reason for it.

In the same vein, I was accused of encouraging commercialism when, at the end of an interview from Spalding, Lincolnshire, with a badly wounded RAF pilot who admitted that his market-garden business was not doing too well, I told listeners, 'If you want any bulbs, why not write to Paul Hart of Spalding'. I had to learn to prevent my heart ruling my head, it seemed.

Fortunately, the programme itself never seemed to suffer from the setbacks and *Have a Go* continued to sail away on the crest of a wave when we were transferred to the old Light Programme. At this time our staunch ally, Barney Colehan, who had been such a help in the show's formative years, moved on to other ventures: Barney has now left the successful TV show *Its A Knockout*, but remains with the BBC in Manchester and one of broadcasting's most respected figures. Violet Carson too went her way and we formed a new team which featured 'Mabel at the table' as the catchphrase soon became. With Stephen Williams as presenter, Joan Archer as assistant producer and Harry Hudson at the piano, we formed a group which stayed together for sixteen years, and I can quite honestly say that during that time there was never a cross word between us. In a business where even a month's perfect harmony between the central figures is almost a rarity, our relationship was really extraordinary.

This was also the start of the television age, when any self-respecting performer was anxious to use the new medium. Naturally we jumped at the chance to do BBC TV's *Ask Pickles*, a simple request show with lots of fun and games. Some wanted to jump on a trampoline—we provided it. A little girl wanted a horse of her very own—we got one. But mind you, not without finding out if her family could provide a stable and a field. We were lucky enough to get Pat Smythe, the first darling of the show-jumping fans, to present the horse to young Elizabeth. I do not think I have ever seen a child so delighted in my life.

And then there was the occasion when one little girl wanted to ride on an elephant. As she was very young, Mabel decided that she would join her and hold her from the back. So the show went out with Mabel sitting astride the elephant displaying rather a lot of nice nylon-covered leg (Mabel has very good legs by the way). When the programme was over she asked the producer, Brian Tesler, 'How did the elephant bit go?', and with a smile spreading across his face he replied: 'Why, was there an elephant?'

With *Have a Go* still topping the charts on radio and *Ask Pickles* doing the same on TV, life was pretty rosy. In 1951 I was awarded the *Daily Mail*'s silver microphone award as radio's most outstanding personality, an award which was repeated three years later when *Ask Pickles* was voted the most entertaining programme. At the time I was also acting in films and the theatre, making guest appearances here, there and everywhere, so there was little chance of relaxation. I often wonder, if I had been a younger man today, what the next logical step would have been, perhaps a chat show host: it's what everyone else seems to become these days!

Have a Go continued for another ten years. Throughout this period there was talk of transferring it to television, a move which I strongly resisted as it was basically a show to listen to, not look at. The pretty girl described by me on radio would not look quite so attractive when seen on TV. The funny old lady with a fund of stories always *sounded* like someone the listener knew. If they saw her it would spoil the illusion. The various regional accents throughout the country were of prime importance too. Again, noting that a Cornishman was 6 ft 2 in and wore a flowered shirt would detract from the way he spoke.

I still think my judgement was sound. Today's TV quiz shows are certainly entertaining, but most rely on a too-similar format with set competitions which need much research and sophisticated presentation. *Have a Go* needed few props. It relied on the participants themselves to provide the humour and pathos: I was certainly not armed with a stack of gags with which to greet each contestant. Spontaneity was always the keynote; from a cleaning lady to a bishop, no one was ever quite sure who would turn up or what they might say.

And I feel too that I was quite right in deciding when the programme had had its day just over ten years ago. Oh, I was still being stopped by people in the street with appreciative comments but, instead of saying such things as, 'I did enjoy your show last week', now they told me, 'My father, God rest his soul, never missed one of your programmes'! I knew then that it was time to move on.

7 TO WALK WITH KINGS

The success of *Have a Go* meant that, for a while, virtually every door was open to me, and I mixed with famous people of all kinds, stars of stage and screen, politicians, eminent businessmen and artists. I'm most proud, of course, of the two royal command performances in which I was invited to take part, one on my own and one with Mabel at the London Coliseum and the Opera House, Blackpool.

Even more interesting for us was a special version of *Have a Go*, given for the Windsor Castle staff. Peter Brough, the excellent ventriloquist of *Educating Archie* fame, organised the entertainment which included our very good friend Beryl Reid. As we came together in the reception room of the castle before the show Beryl said in her usual forthright way: 'Ee, we do meet in some funny places, don't we?'. The mini-show went off very well indeed, with the staff proving most forthcoming and the Royal Family joining in the fun, laughing heartily if one of the bolder participants 'knocked' the Windsor establishment. Afterwards Her Majesty was most charming to us all and Prince Philip expressed a particular pleasure in seeing how *Have a Go* was put together.

It would be all too easy for such occasions to go to any performer's head, but, rest assured, that should anyone start to become too big for his or her boots, there's always someone there to cut him down to size, even in an unintentional way. Some years ago Mabel and I were delighted to be asked to lunch on the terrace of the House of Commons with Sir Harold Wilson, Sir Herbert Morrison, Lord and Lady Shawcross and Lord and Lady Robens, after which occasion Alf Robens became a particular friend. In 1976 he was asked to be the subject of the *With Great Pleasure* series on BBC Radio 4, giving his selection of favourite poems and prose. I felt very pleased when asked to read the extracts and the little programme was quite well received. However, Alf told me afterwards that, when he had told the production girl that he would like me to be his reader, without any mention of my supposed histrionic ability, she turned round and said, 'Oh yes, he talks just like you doesn't he?'

Well, that's not such a bad recommendation, I suppose. And another Yorkshireman who wouldn't be ashamed of 'talking just like me' would, I suspect, be that literary giant, J. B. Priestley. Ever since a boy I had cherished Priestley's works, and after meeting the man later on in life, I admired him all the more. I like his blunt forthrightness, his courage and sincerity in sticking to honestly held opinions that may be unpopular and which may be used against him. I have known him difficult and rather pompous at times, but he is soon restored to favour when I pick up one of his articles or essays.

I often recall a story he told years ago which always makes me chuckle. It is simple, straightforward and true, and all the better for telling in Priestley's gruff, pouting, almost affronted manner. We were in Leeds at the time talking about plays, pantomimes and home life when he mentioned that he and his wife had taken on a new cook-housekeeper and her husband. Priestley stuffed a plug of tobacco firmly into the well burned bowl of his pipe, struck a match and held it aflame as he went on: 'We-ell, as you know, whenever you get a man-and-wife team like this, one always works better than the other. But we made him into a butler and togged him out in a tail coat one evening when we had some friends coming.' Just a hint of a grin creased J.B.'s face. Every-

95

thing had gone well, it seems, until the new butler asked one of the guests: 'Would you like a sweet?'

'No thanks, I prefer cheese', came the reply.

The butler held his ground, hesitating, then 'Aye, that's the trouble', he said. 'You see, we're not very flush for cheese.'

It has always struck me as rather odd that Priestley, who is so interested in people, should be subject to spells of boredom and irritability. One lunchtime in Manchester, for instance, when several of us from the BBC had got together at a pub in Piccadilly, Priestley noticed that a young producer was buying drinks for a second time. 'You're throwing your money around, aren't you?' he called brusquely.

The producer laughed and said: 'Oh, it's all right. Expenses and all that! "To entertaining Mr Priestley . . .!" '

There was a spasm of laughter from the rest which died on their lips as Priestley frowned and said in a tone of sullen sombreness: 'But, I'm not being entertained!'

On another occasion, during the recording of one of Priestley's superb 'Postscript' broadcasts in a basement studio at 200, Oxford Street, London—bastion of much of the BBC's wartime broadcasting to Overseas—J.B. heard the engineer refer to him as a gas-bag, and promptly left the studio. A senior member of the staff managed to placate him and was conducting him back to the studio when, to add injury to insult, the Security man insisted on checking Mr Priestley's pass which he'd already examined not ten minutes before. You can imagine the reception this was given!

The rank or station of people never worries this courageous battler. He has never thought much of the circuitous ways of officialdom, just as he is inclined to scorn the pin-striped proprieties of the over-cautious public servant. Yet, for all his great and powerful qualities, I always see in him the ambitious boy who has got on through his own talents and intends that everyone should recognise this fact.

I like the story of the literary sycophant who gushingly approached him at a party with: 'Oh, Mr Priestley, I think *Angel Pavement* is the most wonderful thing that's ever been written!'

He fixed his admirer with a glare. 'Is that so? What's the matter with *The Good Companions*?'

There is very little wrong with *The Good Companions*, as J.B. is only too well aware. Indeed, he often feels that it has overshadowed much of his other work in people's estimation with no just cause. A few years ago, Trevor Hill, the BBC Manchester-based producer with whom I have worked many times and who has very kindly supplied a postscript to this book, rang to say that Priestley's agent had turned down a request from the BBC to do a reading of *The Good Companions*. Could I lend a persuasive voice? I was happy to be able to do so and, a few days later, could not help playing a small trick when ringing up to tell the Great Man's personal reaction. 'Read on, dear boy, read on!' I pronounced in a passable imitation of the Master's voice. Read on we did and the reading proved a great success, with *Angel Pavement* following.

Despite his aggressive, glowering exterior, Priestley is a sensitive man with a talent for putting thoughts and feelings into simple, easily understood language. As I write this I have just heard that he has been awarded the Order of Merit for his work for literature. As the finest writer of our generation, not only of novels, but plays and essays, he is certainly worthy of this honour. I should like to offer him my sincere congratulations.

Another irascible character who had a great deal to offer was Gilbert Harding, the plain-speaking, enormously intelligent broadcaster who made a lasting impression as one of the original *What's My Line* panellists. He quickly gained a reputation for being rude and ill-tempered, a reputation which he admitted was true to a point, although he also pointed out that he was never deliberately cold or bad-mannered with people who did not deserve his spleen. He was very accustomed to incidents such as the one when a well-dressed woman accosted him in a restaurant with the words, 'Are you going to give me your autograph, or are you going to be rude to me?'

'Neither', he replied simply.

Yet he did quarrel with many people, particularly women with whom he frequently did not feel at ease. Very often he merely behaved like a rather spoilt small boy, saying things for effect which he didn't really mean. Later, there would be some sort of wordless apology, usually a bunch of flowers.

Gilbert hated prejudice. He was once talking to a group of coloured US soldiers in a pub near an air base when a white GI walked in and whispered something to the blackmen who immediately left. Naturally Gilbert was furious. 'Listen bud', said the soldier, 'How would you feel if one of those chaps raped your favourite girl?'

'I should be very happy for her', Harding retorted, 'And so would she!'

His ready wit was matched by his use of language, but though scrupulously correct he was never a pedant. One story which he liked to tell illustrates this point exactly. Apparently Dr Webster, the famous American dictionary compiler, was caught by his wife as he cuddled the maid on a settee.

'Dr Webster, I am surprised', the good lady exclaimed.

'No my dear' he corrected gently. 'I am surprised. You are astonished!'

Gilbert was equally happy with a good story against himself or things which he held dear. A good Catholic, he was fond of the tale of a young man who offered to convert to Catholicism in order to marry the girl he loved. On his first attendance at mass, he assiduously followed all the twists and turns of the service, genuflecting and crossing himself far more times than necessary. At one point, so frantic were his contortions that the girl turned to him and said urgently, 'Are your flies open?'

'No', he replied, 'Should they be?'

Another sharp wit who also often delighted in sweeping aside pretence was Sir Compton Mackenzie, who appeared at one publisher's lunch for all the world like the Scarlet Pimpernel in middle age, with his sharp, formidable face and neat goatee beard, and a deceptively light-hearted approach that gave the impression he was out to make a jamboree of the occasion. He stood up to speak, grinned sheepishly and then worked himself up into such a verbal frenzy that he completely forgot that Herbert Morrison, the chairman for the occasion, to whom he was proposing a toast, had left early on official business. With a dramatically searching glance along the table, he set eyes on me and exclaimed: 'I know what we'll do! Let's offer a toast to Wilfred Pickles, and I can honestly say I have not missed even one of his "Have a Go" programmes.' It was a delightful tribute and I later found Compton Mackenzie a most entertaining man, rich in humorous anecdotes and faith in ordinary people. In his character there seemed to be all the Frenchman's animation, the fiery stubbornness of the Scot, and none of the archness of the literary set.

My own previous scribblings, while with little claim for artistic merit, had been fun and awarded both Mabel and myself much pleasure. I like to think the public experienced some enjoyment too! The luncheon given in the Dorchester Hotel by Christina Foyle of the famous booksellers to launch my autobiography, *Between You and Me*, was one of the most terrifying moments of my life, as I entered the ornate and luxurious room where these bookish operations are organised each month. The hundreds of people sitting at numbered tables seemed to be expecting something superbly witty and extravagantly brilliant. I felt so impossibly small, especially when I set eyes on the scarlet-jacketed toastmaster, that I wanted to shrink back into the obscurity of Greater London and write nothing more incriminating than anonymous letters to the local papers.

Near us at the long top table was the Bishop of London, an optimistic, amiable man with laughter-wrinkles round his eyes, and Lady Astor, voluble and full of mischievous fun. When her turn came to speak she immediately leaned into the microphone and, with a piece of subtle leg-pulling, had everybody with her. She took the starch out of the occasion and had us rocking in admiring merriment at her astuteness as she analysed the American accent. This was the main part of her theme, a follow-up to a generous comment on my own news-reading work. She ended up by gazing first at me and then at the Bishop of London with that stern, no-nonsense expression of hers, and then saying solemnly that she had pleasure in supporting ' . . . these goodly, Godly—and entirely mercenary—men!'

When we first met, face to face, after the speech, with a reproving twinkle in those eyes that were at once gay and serious, Lady Astor remarked: 'They tell me, Pickles, that you have strong views politically?' It was a fair question, so I gave her a straight answer.

'Naturally, I have my views, but I'm not a party man.'

Lady Astor wagged a warning finger under my nose. 'Don't let them,' she said, 'don't let them ever make a politician of you. They'll try, you know.'

Well, they never did make a politician of me, although, for a brief period, I did become a journalist. It all began when I met Percy Cudlipp, then editor of the *Daily Herald*, who seemed an integral part of this street of a million stories, where reporters and photographers can be seen frantically hailing taxis, and where the man on the opposite stool in the milk bar might well be a new Boswell and the stranger buying a paper a second Chesterton. Cudlipp was the sort of man you can be frank with, so during a purely social lunch date I began rather provocatively: 'You know, the depression and misery of the people isn't real. It's only in the newspapers!'

'Well, if you're so sure about it, why don't you go out into the country and find this spirit of the people—and write about it, for us?' he replied. 'Nothing political in it. Straight-forward stuff, you know. Write about the people as you find them.'

I jumped at this chance, not only to prove my point, but to look a bit deeper into the lives of the ordinary people than *Have a Go* had allowed me to do. As we set off, Mabel looked at me rather quizzically. 'They'll make a politician of you yet, Pickles', she warned, but I felt then, as I still feel today, that when one has built up public confidence in one sphere it would be taking an unfair advantage to make political use of it. If democracy is to mean anything at all, it must be kept clean and more sincere than some of the noisier politicians would like, and this means that well-known actors and singers and sportsmen, and other non-political person-alities, have less right morally (in the interests of unemotional voting) to shout their heads off on polling day than their admirers and listeners.

This was the sort of formula I was working out in my mind as we struck north east for Ipswich and Yarmouth, our first answer to Percy Cudlipp's challenge. The journey covered Coventry, Tyneside, Hull, the South Wales valleys, the Black Country, the Potteries, Sheffield, the Yorkshire Dales, Lancashire, Glasgow and Edinburgh. We saw Britain at work, at play, and in her home; we met the housewives during the shopping rush and the men at their machines; we talked to a young shepherdess in the Dales and to the cramped families in the shadow of the Gorbals.

Percy Cudlipp was pleased with the way things turned out, and so was I. But there was one blot on these pages of news-print which upset and annoyed me. In the Yorkshire Dales we had come across two Newcastle girls on a camping holiday, both nineteen and only a few months out of school. We discussed the beauty of this part of the world and how good it was to be alive, and then I asked one of them what she would do if she had the power to change something. She pondered for a moment, then replied: 'I would change all Communists into Conservatives.' I put this in my article, but it was not printed, the only deletion in the whole series.

Interviewing has, of course, always been one of my favourite jobs, and another book would be needed to describe just a few of the celebrities and ordinary people to whom I have enjoyed speaking. Not all work, especially broadcasts, ran smoothly however. I still blush to recall one incident in a series which came from various stately homes. The venue was Houghton Towers where James I having enormously enjoyed the dinner served to him, knighted what was left of the round of beef. The scriptwriter, as usual, had visited the family and prepared the programme some weeks in advance of the mobile recording dates.

On the day, Lady Philomena, Sir Cuthbert de Houghton's second wife was interviewed first, but as lunch time approached I had yet to meet the Premier Baronet. It had been quite a long morning without a break and after walking round one wing of the typically Elizabethan 'E'-shaped house, I turned to the scriptwriter and whispered urgently 'Where is it?' One expects understanding friends at a time like that.

'Ah yes,' she replied, instantly finding her bearings and pointing to an oak panelled door. 'It's just in there.'

Shooting through the door, I lurched down an unexpected step to end up facing an elderly gentleman wearing a smoking cap and looking up from his *Financial Times* with an understandably startled expression.

'Oh er . . . I'm Wilfred Pickles' I stammered, hastily adjusting my dress.

'And I'm S-Sir Cuthbert. And t-this is my d-d-DEN', boomed back the Baronet. East and West wings may look alike but the appointment of rooms often differs!'

On a more serious note, one interview I shall also never forget, was with Sir William Penney, the atomic research scientist. Here are his words from a memorable broadcast:

We all faced away from the explosion as the last few seconds were counted over the loudspeakers. Suddenly there was an intense flash, visible all round the horizon. The sight before our eyes was terrifying. A great greyish black cloud being hurled thousands of feet into the air and increasing in size with astonishing rapidity.

Thus did William Penney describe the setting off of Britain's first atom bomb at Montebello in 1952. Recalling his voice as I turned into the car park of the building where I had an appointment with the modest scientist who had found fame overnight, I wondered what sort of man he would turn out to be. Lofty, academic, coldly reasonable? He could have been all these things and I would have excused him. For here was a man who, at the time, had given the country the strongest weapon in her armoury, and with the weapon, a more compelling voice in world affairs.

But I was introduced to a smiling, good-natured, family man in early middle age: a man with a paternal air and a tendency to put on weight round the middle. I was still a little uneasy as to how to begin, as it seemed odd to be asking the most confidential figure in the whole country to talk about himself and his job. Yet, for the next few hours, without any frills, and with a few careful draws at his cigarette as he picked his way round the security-bound episodes, Dr Penney held my attention by simply describing his life and work.

He told me how, with Group Captain Geoffrey Cheshire, VC, he flew behind the team responsible for dropping the first bombs on Nagasaki and saw the spreading mushroom which the whole world was to know and fear. During our talk Sir William rationalised his first impressions and reactions into an attitude that reconciles his scientific realism and his broad humanitarian outlook. 'The atomic bombs did not win the last war,' he said, 'they stopped it.'

In the ensuing peace, two major projects engaged his attention, the development of the civilian application of atomic energy and the making of the first British atom bomb. It was on the morning of 8 October 1952, on the deck of the aircraft carrier *Compania* that William Penney saw that first bomb go off.

When he came back to Britain, over twenty-five years ago, Dr Penney was overwhelmed by reporters, photographers and newsreel cameramen. He satisfied their picture requirements by walking several times from his plane but the reporters couldn't get a word from him. Then he went home to his family. Sir William has always liked the simple life. He is happiest at his own hearth, as demonstrated by the scene that met reporters who called to interview him when he was knighted for his work. Under the door knocker was a note on which he had written: 'One small white, one small brown. Pay you Monday.'

How well I understand his feelings! Perhaps my own love of hearth and home is best summed up in these verses from Arthur Benson's poem, *My Will*:

> I would live, if I had my will,
> in an old stone grange on a Yorkshire hill
> ivy encircled, lichen streaked
> low and mullioned, gable peaked,
> with a velvet lawn and a hedge of yew,
> an apple orchard to saunter through,
> hyacinth scented in spring's clear prime
> and rich with roses in summertime,
> and waft of heather over the hill,
> had I my will

Then when the last guest steps to my side
may it be summer, the windows wide
I would smile as the parson prayed,
smile to think I was once afraid
death should beckon me take my hand,
smile at the door of the silent land,
then the slumber, how good to sleep
under the grass where the shadows creep,
where the headstones slant on the windswept hill!
I shall have my will!

8   FRIENDS AND NEIGHBOURS

If I were to look back and try to pinpoint the best and most enduring thing that ever happened to me, it could only be that, whilst having a life full of incident, mingling with celebrities from all walks of life, I have always drawn strength from my roots in ordinary folk and continued to gain the greatest pleasure from conversation with these same people.

Now, having travelled the world, I am happy to remain in this country. For health reasons I have made my home at Brighton among Hilaire Belloc's 'great hills of the South Country', and I can well understand the emotion which prompted him to write:

> I never get between the pines
> But I smell the Sussex air;
> Nor I ever come on a belt of sand,
> But my home is there.

Yet my heart will always remain, with Arthur Benson, in my native North Country. For a long time I feared that regionalism, the dialects, the pulse of the north was bound to die. Every modern-age development pointed towards it: greater centralisation in most things, the disturbing fashion in which frankness was mistaken for bad manners, and of course, as already discussed the BBC, whose previous demand for Oxford English made my own brand of the language rather revolutionary.

Now I am not so sure that the north needs any crusaders on

its behalf. It is just as strong, individualistic and original today as it ever was. It has survived the worst of the impact of standardisation and one can't help feeling that it has become so clear that whilst you can put a veneer on a worthless pebble, diamonds can still look rough. The inventiveness is still there and the drollery, and the refreshing honesty that has no time for diplomacy.

A perfect example of this is the story of the two mates from Leeds who went for a drink together every evening, always following the same routine, ending with 'Goodnight. See thee in 'tmorning' on parting. On one particular day, the younger man went round to his neighbour and asked his wife if Fred were in.

'I'm afraid there's no use in seeing him', she replied. 'He passed away in the night.'

'O aye'. He registered no surprise. 'Did he say owt about a pot o' paint?'

Understatement is almost a way of life in Yorkshire. Ever cautious in all their dealings, Yorkshire people seem to try to make everyone else aware of some impending doom. 'Be good', they exhort each other on parting, 'Behave thiself'. Yet their open-heartedness with strangers is legendary. Broad vowels and brusque speech are possibly useful in cloaking a warm interior. In a region where swear words are accepted as everyday adjectives, with little or no venom behind them, it may seem odd to a stranger that everyone, from the shop assistant to the vicar, is referred to as 'love'. How well I remember seeing a family trailing up from the beach at Blackpool, one young child with sand in his shoes crying as he refused to go another step further.

'Oh come on, bloody love', his exasperated mother shouted at him.

A northerner's speech does indeed reflect his character. Unpretentious, economical people with little literary or oratorical ambitions frequently use language more pithily than their more florid neighbours. In dismissing someone who talks a lot without getting to the point, a Lancastrian will say 'He talks and sez nowt'. And, borrowing the analogy of the market place, a Yorkshireman will sum up even his best friend's faults, without bitterness or rancour, in the simple phrase, 'he's nowt a pound, and bumpin' weight at that!'

Somehow, and I don't think I'm being simplistic here, life is more *definite* in the north, black and white, right and wrong are clearly distinguished. Admittedly, the good don't always prosper, but those on the make do seem to get their come-uppance with amazing regularity. Take, for instance, the farmer who married a wealthy widow. Everybody knew that he married her because she had a lot of money but, as their relationship developed, she not only had the money but also had the whip hand. Two neighbouring farmers discussing the situation together were responsible for the telling, if I-told-you-so phrase, 'Ah well, it's his own fault, he married midden for't muck and now he's fair bothered wi't stink.'

The Yorkshireman's love of his 'brass' is well-known. Of course, this characteristic has been somewhat exaggerated in music-hall jokes, yet I can vouch for the truth of the story of the wit from Bradford who, hearing the local children singing the carol 'While Shepherds watched their flocks by night', came out with 'And considering the price of wool these days there's no wonder they watched 'em'.

Yet I wouldn't go so far as to substantiate the following tale of the Yorkshireman's desire to get his money's worth at all costs. Rumour hath it that in the middle of a riotous farmers' dinner at Skipton, one member of the company leaned over to another to point out that his next-door neighbour seemed a bit quiet. 'He's been dead for twenty minutes' came back the reply, 'but I'm not going to spoil a good do'!

A glimmer of truth, perhaps, but what I do know is that, if the north country man strikes a hard bargain in times of plenty, he is at his most resourceful—and astonishingly humorous—in times of adversity. Today's troubled economic times often bring back to me the dark days of the thirties' trade slump when the industrial north was hit very badly, just as the Lancashire manufacturing towns are today. I remember, in particular, one journey Mabel and I made through that part of the country then, when mills were closing down one after another every week. We travelled through Preston and on to Blackburn. From a hill we looked down onto the valley of mill chimneys. No reassuring spirals of smoke issued from most of them, and from where we were Blackburn looked like a town of the dead.

It was the same in nearby Rishton—unemployment, underemployment and low wages counted in shillings for those weavers lucky enough still to be at their looms. One of the men I spoke to in this depressed little township stood on the corner of the main street not far from the parish church and cricket ground in their pretty rural setting. 'Things are really bad, owd lad', he said, 'Even t'rats'll hev nowt to live on 'ere in a bit!'

The phrase stuck in my mind as we drove on through the industrial desolation of east Lancashire. I marvelled at the courage of these people and was moved by their rather grim humour, a rich streak of which appeared during the depression. It was characteristic that most of their jokes had their core in the dole. One of them I have ever since regarded as a gem. I heard it in Great Harwood—known as 'Arrod' to the locals, an urban district on the road to nowhere. A young weaver told me the story about an incident at the Labour Exchange, when an unemployed man walked up to the counter to sign on. He had a dog with him and the clerk leaned over the counter and said: 'That's a nice Corgi you have there.'

'Nay, it's a greyhound', said the signer-on.

'But—it's legs aren't long enough for a greyhound, surely.'

'They were when I started looking for a job!'

I was amazed by the friendliness, kindliness, generosity and humour of these sociable Lancastrians. And it's perhaps because that county has never been as prosperous as its neighbouring Yorkshire, that so much adversity has produced a rich fund of folk humour, prose and poetry. One of my own favourites is Samuel Laycock's *Welcome Bonny Brid*, written during the cotton famine of 1861 when he was out of work and his wife had just produced their third child. Here are four verses:

> Tha'rt welcome, little bonny brid,
> But shouldn't ha' come just when tha did;
>   Times are bad
> We're short o' pobbies for our Joe,
> But that, of course, tha didn't know,
>   Did ta, lad?
>
> God bless thi, love! aw'm fain tha'rt come,
> Just try and mak' thisel awhoam:
>   Here's thi nest;
> Tha'rt like thi mother to a tee,
> But tha's thi feyther's nose, aw see,
>   Well, aw'm blest!
>
> Thi feyther's noan been wed so lung,
> An' yet tha sees he's middlin' thrung
>   Wi' yo' all
> Besides thi little brother Ted,
> We've one upsteers, asleep i' bed,
>   Wi' our Joe.
>
> But tho' we've childer two or three,
> We'll mak' a bit o' room for thee,
>   Bless thee, lad!
> Tha'rt th' prattiest brid we have i'th' nest,
> So hutch up closer to mi breast;
>   I'm thi dad.

When a southerner goes north, he usually fails to detect any difference between Lancashire and Yorkshire. He would not

see in, say, the Halifax Building Society, a symbol of difference. But its massive pillars and aura of prosperity are as
Yorkshire as the Dales. The old Roses' rivalry between the
two counties is never better focused than when the north of
England's own 'test matches' are played at Headingley or
Old Trafford. And, however much I may have conceded to
the Lancastrian as far as personal characteristics are concerned, I am still a loyal Yorkshire cricket follower.

How droll is the humour at these cricketing feasts! How
revealing the expressions on the ring of faces as you scan the
perimeter of the pitch! Hundreds of picnics; flasks, sand-
wiches, buckets of tea. Knotted handkerchiefs on the men's
heads. Dapper business men in their shirt sleeves, murmur-
ing advice to get on with it or change the attack. The following story, I think, illustrates the intense domestic nature
of the matches better than any photographs or descriptive
accounts.

A southerner watching a Roses' game applauded a neat
stroke by a batsman.

'Oh, well played, sir!' he exclaimed.

The stocky fellow on his felt turned and asked: 'Dosta
belong to Lancashire?'

'No', said the visitor.

From his right came the query: 'Dosta come fra' Yorkshire?' 'No', he said.

Both his neighbours looked at him and said: 'Well, mind
thi own ruddy business then!'

Such partisanship could well have been levelled at that
great Tyke, fast-bowler Fiery Fred Trueman, whose temper
on and off the field was legendary. I'm sure Fred won't mind
my repeating a story told by two old ladies who were once
his next-door neighbours. Gathering that all was not well in
the Trueman household, the sisters postponed asking if they
could borrow the cricketer's lawnmower. When peace had
apparently prevailed, they plucked up courage to make their

demand, and at once the mower came hurtling over the hedge towards them. Fearing to touch it after this display, they retreated, only to see minutes later their very obliging neighbour cutting the lawn for them with the machine which he had so kindly loaned!

With Fred actions spoke louder than words. Many Yorkshire players seem a mixture of arrogance and caution, characteristics which are certainly shown by the county's most outstanding player of recent years, Geoffrey Boycott. And the same tenacity, combined with exceedingly literal interpretation of the truth at all times, has always run through the side. There is a much-repeated anecdote concerning the great Wilfred Rhodes and George Hirst who were cheated from achieving an easy victory over Middlesex at Lords by the vagaries of the English summer. After a variable Saturday in which little play was possible, the two men were walking the next day in Regent's Park in blazing sunshine. Said Hirst wistfully: 'If it had been a day like this yesterday we'd have had 'em out by half past twelve.'

'Nay George', corrected Wilfred, 'Quarter to one, quarter to one.'

It is this same sense of community, of belonging to a recognisable group, that has always impressed me about the Jewish race. I have always admired their sense of humour—the ability to make jokes against themselves—and especially their love of family life. My greatest friend today, Jack Apel, is a Jew. We want nothing from each other, nor do we ask anything of each other. But I know that if I asked him to fetch me a toothpick from the furthest inch of Asia he would do his best to get it for me and I would do the same for him.

Jack would appreciate the story of the Jewish maiden ladies who had devoted their lives to their parents, never marrying. The two sisters were sitting by the bed of their dying father who rallied occasionally from his slumber. On one occasion he said: 'Don't forget Fred Riley owes me twenty pounds', and the eldest daughter said: 'Sensible to the last.'

The old man dozed off again, then rallied again to say: 'Don't forget I owe Fred Fairclough seventy-five pounds.'

'He's rambling again', she exclaimed!

One of the most interesting people I ever met was also a Jew, Jacob Lewis Fine. The importance of people like Jack—as he was known to his friends—Fine in these times is that through his personal experiences run many modern major themes, such as political persecution, racial discrimination, escape to freedom, exploitation, impoverishment and trade union organisation. A political refugee, Fine fled from Russia to the one country where he knew he could live in freedom, England. In almost reverential tones he told me: 'I shall never forget my first sight of Tower Bridge. I did not know then what the bridge was, but I suddenly saw two great arms between the tall towers rise up and I felt that this great structure was a deliberate gesture of welcome, a symbol of British asylum to the homeless, friendless people who sought refuge.'

Destined to be a leader of the Jewish clothing workers in East London, eventually becoming secretary of their trade union, Jacob was greatly responsible for unifying the Jewish workers with the Gentiles, bringing about the amalgamation of their separate trade union organisations. A naturalised English subject, he was awarded the Order of the British Empire for public services rendered in, as he would say with pride, '. . . Stepney, . . . my Stepney. Since the day I first came there to live I have loved the area'.

Illustrative of Fine's general attitude to Britain is an incident that happened when he was speaking at a large gathering. At question time a man got up and, pointing at Jacob, asked: 'Can that man tell us what his nationality is?' From his manner it was clear that he regarded Fine as a foreigner who shouldn't be part of public affairs in this country. The enormous East London audience must have sensed how deeply affected was the neat little man with a slightly foreign accent who insisted on answering personally the challenge flung at him.

'Today', Jack Fine said, 'I am a British subject, thank God. And perhaps I am a better Britisher than is my friend who asked the question, for you see he is British simply because he was born in this country, but I am British by choice.'

Britain did well to open Tower Bridge and admit such a man, as it did to admit many of his fellow refugees. And so, to all my Jewish friends, I greet you—Shalom Aleichem.

Jacob Fine found his chosen land. I, and countless many others, are lucky in that we have always belonged to one nation, one region, 'our patch', that particular spot on the map where we were born. For, whatever reservations I may express about character traits, however much I may rail against or gently chide my fellow North Countrymen, deep down I am, and will remain, proud to be a Yorkshireman.

It's a feeling found everywhere amongst Yorkshire folk, at home and abroad, expressed most amusingly in the story of the father and his eight-year-old son who were stopped by a stranger in York and asked to be directed to the well-known Shambles area of the old town. After the father had given directions, the little lad looked at the stranger and asked: 'Do you belong to Yorkshire?'

'No,' he replied, 'I'm a stranger in these parts.'

As they parted company the father gave his son a clout. 'Never let me hear you ask such a daft question again.'

'Why?' queried the lad.

'Why? If a chap comes from Yorkshire he'll tell you before you've time to ask him, and if he doesn't, don't embarrass him!'

Trevor Hill, who provides the final word for this book, is a southerner by birth but certainly a northerner by adoption, having worked and lived in Manchester for many years now.

I'm sure the north has adopted him as well as he has taken to it. What more then is there for me to say, except to round off as I did some twenty-five years ago when reading the news: 'Goodnight everybody. And to all northerners, wherever you may be, Goodneet.'

POSTSCRIPT

by
Trevor Hill
(Senior Producer, Network Radio, BBC Manchester)

There's quite a lot in this book which the author doesn't say about himself, for within a reasonably holy trinity exists the *Have A Go* person, the actor person and the person whose life away from all the brouhaha of publicity usually associated with stars of radio, television and the stage has always remained a private affair.

I first came face to face with the already legendary Wilfred Pickles in that waiting-room at the old BBC studios in Piccadilly, Manchester, the scene of his beginnings in broadcasting. But it was now August, 1949. He'd just popped in to give an encouraging word to a very young Billie Whitelaw who, like Wilfred, was about to do a play reading for the no-nonsense Nan Macdonald, the Organiser of Northern Children's Hour. When the BBC Regions opened up again at the end of the War it was Nan who branched out with a quite different approach to the sort of programmes which young people would hear. And in entertaining them, she also won over a very large portion of the adult population as well. Not for her a version of *Have a Go* in her programme schedule, so Wilfred's contracts were for his appearances in her remarkable output of plays and features. Everyone knew the voice of *Have a Go* but how many listeners could even begin to identify the person who was behind the character of 'Prince Rupert', or that really evil German villain in the current serial, the toothless old grandfather or a sleepy dormouse?

And it was a very different person again who went out with the North Region mobile recording unit on *Walks With Wilfred* scripted in the early days by Joan Littlewood before the theatre whisked her away. No Yorkshire Fells shepherd or stonemason was asked 'Are ye courtin'?' or about their most embarrassing moments, but rather how they coped with winter snows, and looked upon nature that could be both cruel and kind.

Wilfred's face wore a big smile as he joked and chatted with Billie Whitelaw, putting her at her ease, giving her hints and tips on the character she was about to play. But as I watched them in that waiting-room, I wondered how he and I would get on together when he discovered that a young BBC producer—and a southerner at that—had been sent up to Manchester, whilst an apparently tireless and sometimes tiresome Programme Organiser was sent on three months' leave to give herself and the staff a rest.

Such was Wilfred's allegiance to Nan Macdonald that on our first meeting he simply said, 'Perhaps I won't do quite so much whilst she's away. You understand.'

I'd already been told that nothing was ever allowed to interfere with Wilfred Pickles' work for Northern Children's Hour. Other departments, other producers may have offered bigger parts, larger contracts, but here was a man who kept faith. Miss Dora Broom of no 2, Railway Sidings, Douglas, Isle of Man could never get over the fact that *the* Wilfred Pickles always read her delightful *Matilda Mouse* stories, not just for the North but throughout the whole British Isles, besides being heard by listeners in America, Canada, Australia and other English-speaking countries via the BBC's Transcription Service.

When Nan Macdonald decided to leave the North altogether to work in London, her successor took up an idea for a new radio series—*Afternoon Out*, visits to English stately homes open to the public—from my wife, Margaret Potter a free-lance script writer. Margaret had already written several things for Wilfred including adapting the part of Lewis Carroll's 'Gryphon' for a special 1951 Festival of Britain Light Programme musical version of *Alice In Wonderland* and *Through The Looking Glass*. His reading of the Jobberwocky poem set to music is one of the treasures in the BBC archives.

At that recording session, Wilfred, hearing the theme song, asked me about the vocalist. It was Jimmy Young who, at that time, sang for Ray Martin, conductor of the BBC Northern Variety Orchestra. I'd spent every Friday evening for several months before *Alice* sharing my announcer's mike with Jimmy. Being closeted together in the small space between the doors of Studio 1 gave Ray Martin the right sort of 'separation' he wanted between the orchestra and his vocalists.

And now Ray, who'd composed the score for our musical, decided he wanted Wilfred too 'on separation'. So, for the sake of technical perfection, Wilfred spoke his lines in one BBC studio at Maida Vale, London, and the large orchestra, with George Mitchell and the Mitchell Maids, were in another studio. At the same recording session the chorus parts were scored precisely one seventh of an octave below that of the key signature and recorded on their own. When speeded up that seventh we arrived at tiny oyster voices pleading 'Will you, won't you, will you, won't you join the dance?'

In fact, *Adventurers in Wonderland* became an exercise in technical 'separation'. The 'White Queen' who was being played by Jeanne De Casalis in her 'Mrs Feather' voice— ('What is one and one andoneandoneandone?') and the 'White Knight' as portrayed by Jimmy Edwards ('Ah! A Glor-rious vic-tory was it not?') were being shunted around different studios and acoustics to such an extent that Wilfred was heard to declare in a witch-like voice, 'When shall we three meet again?'

When Wilfred began his broadcasting career, the BBC in Manchester used an enormous Thorneycroft pantechnicon for mobile recording and broadcasting. It had a studio in the front end and two disc recorders bolted down at the back— they were laughingly called portable! Disc recording was still widely used, at this time on 78 rpm besides the large 'Slow Speed' acetate discs on which you could record up to fifteen minutes or so, despite the fact that as far back as 1924, the Vox Gramophone Company had a dictating machine which used a steel wire. The batteries used for powering the equipment could be charged as the huge vehicle journeyed through the North of England and Scotland. Certain humped-back bridges in the Yorkshire Wolds and in parts of Cumberland were noted as being 'impassable for recording purposes'.

During wartime, whilst working in the Programme Engineering Department on the BBC's Overseas services, I'd been used to a form of recording onto large spools of steel tape. The Philips-Miller process used film, a stylus cutting into the emulsion—but nothing *looked* as exciting as this gleaming machine with its two large reels of steel tape whipping through the works. In order to keep the correct tension and prevent 'wow', the steel tape went into baths of mercury which, in turn, either slowed down or speeded up the driving motors and with the lights turned out in the Recording Channel, there would be a wonderful display of electrical blue flashes as the tape made contact with the mercury. A break in the tape wasn't a matter of a bit of sticky and scissors but rather the excitement of donning a pair of goggles and doing a spot-welding job right there and then.

In Hamburg with Forces Broadcasting shortly after the war ended, I came across the German magnetofonband or plastic tape-recorder. These small portable machines—and they really were portable—were the kind used by the German Corps of Signals. The recording quality wasn't a patch on the then current BBC disc recording onto acetate blanks, but for Outside Broadcast use, with a magnetic tape system you had no stylus or cutting head jumping with vibration off the surface of the record when recording 'on the hoof'. Somehow, the BBC's recording engineers had achieved the almost impossible with Wynford Vaughan Thomas and others as they recorded their commentaries from lurching Wellingtons over Berlin—but then, they were the experts.

The Magnetophoneband came to the rescue the day after the Berlin Airlift began. Plane space was far too valuable to allow me to take a recording engineer to operate a conventional disc recorder, so I had half an hour of intensive tuition from a German engineer in Hamburg on the magic box, then went off to meet two of my Forces Broadcasting colleagues who were both hoping to get into the BBC: Cliff Michelmore and Raymond Baxter took it in turns to work the machine and to do the interviews for the feature.

Working as a civilian once again meant returning to disc recording but now, instead of lumbering pantechnicons reduced to a speed limit of 20 mph, the BBC image of the 1950s was enhanced by shining Humber-Pullman recording cars and a corps of very expert Recording Engineers. Today, often just a producer or interviewer with a mono or stereo Uher tape machine turns up for a programme, such has been the technical progress on the sound recording side. Even the light-weight Video colour recorders for mobile Television recording weigh far less than some of the microphone stands of early days. And on the subject of microphones, still essential in the world of sound, I wonder if the young announcer, Wilfred Pickles, remembered to use that small hammer which hung at the side of the carbon granule microphone in order to tap the mike. This made for far better sound reproduction as it shook the granules up. It must have shaken many a listener too if he first switched on, *then* tapped!

Margaret and I were to meet Wilfred and Mabel frequently with *Afternoon Out*. The basic idea behind the programme was that Wilfred should link 'actuality' recordings made at the historic houses, with studio reconstructions of scenes from the past enacted by a studio cast. This was the same series in which he had an embarrassing encounter with the owner of Houghton Towers described earlier. One March day in 1954 we collected them from their imposing house in Disley, Cheshire, later to become the home of *Coronation Street*'s Elsie Tanner, Pat Phoenix, after the Pickles decided to live permanently in London. Wilfred had tried the 'Rolls Royce' image but soon discarded it.

'Seems a bit daft, me an' a whacking great Rolls. If we carry on like this we'll be visiting Night Clubs next!'

On this occasion we were on our way to meet the Earl and Countess of Derby, not the father for whom Wilfred had donned evening dress as an embryo announcer, but his son who now resided at Knowsley Hall, Prescott. The Knowsley visit sticks in my mind for two reasons. First, the Earl of Derby was having some alterations made to the house and a new exterior wall was being built the day we arrived to record so a gang of bricklayers were hard at work.

'Ow do', Wilfred called in typical greeting. The voice and face were immediately recognised and soon a grinning band of brickies were chatting with him.

'Like to lay a brick for us, Wilfred?' asked one of the younger men.

'W-e-l-l . . . yes, I might at that'.

There was a general nudging and winking as Mabel took his coat. In a good humoured sort of way, some rather hoped to see him lay an egg, but those expressions quickly changed as a practised hand and expert eye took up a brick, tossed it to judge the precise weight with one hand whilst the other set down just the right amount of mortar, laid the brick, tapped to level and, with a final flourish, removed the surplus and neatly pointed at one and the same time. This six-or seven-second performance was accompanied by just about the most nonchalant whistling I've ever heard.

Many an artist becomes used to signing all manner of bits of paper down to sweet wrappers but I doubt if anyone else has been asked to autograph a brick. It was, believe it or not, presented some time later that day whilst we were recording inside the house. The Earl's butler, Davis, brought in the object of the workmen's affections on a silver salver and enquired 'If Mr Pickles would kindly autograph and lay this one'.

Lord Derby had taken a very keen interest in the programme right from the start, making pertinent suggestions regarding those who might be interviewed, and what scenes from the family past might go well in dramatised form. But it was the Countess who noticed the words 'Background of Conversation During Dinner' on Wilfred's copy of the script. If we didn't have a large enough studio cast, then this sort of thing would be played in from an effects record for the scene which depicted the opening dinner in the State Dining Room at Knowsley in 1821.

'Can't we be the guests?' she asked, and within a short space of time, the Earl and Countess of Derby, Lord Roseberry, Mrs Gerald Legge and the rest of the Knowsley houseparty were in that State Dining Room doing a 'rent-a-crowd'. Perhaps the word 'rhubarb' *was* a little more prominent than I'd have wished for but it was a most enjoyable recording for all concerned, not least the star. It is surprising how many leading ladies and gentlemen in Radio drama never stir from their seats for 'Crowd' effects. Not so Mr Pickles who, ten to one, has looked up the period in which the action takes place and worked out precisely what would be appropriate 'rhubarb' for the occasion.

No two people are the same, which makes the pattern of broadcasting life all the richer yet, with the exception of a certain few who seem determined to tell him dirty stories which they imagine he will repeat, Wilfred invariably appears to be at home and at ease with almost everyone. He meets and talks to them professionally and socially on their level, but it has always been interesting to observe how people react before meeting him. Being interviewed is in itself something of an experience. Who doesn't wish to be seen and heard at their best? To be interviewed by Wilfred Pickles added another dimension.

'He won't be too—er—familiar, will he?' asked one nervous rather than pompous official. 'I shall, of course, call him *Mr* Pickles!'

Fair enough and we would warn Mr Pickles that a little formality was expected, as we set up for the recording. As soon as we started, the interviewee would positively beam with genuine delight and say 'How are you Wilfred. Welcome to our town, Wilfred. Is Mabel with you, Wilfred?'

Wilfred is an excellent listener, an essential qualification not only for a top interviewer, but also for an actor. If the interviewer is only interested in what *he* is going to say next, or *how* he is going to say it, then he's in the wrong profession. The actor too has listened, listened carefully to many voices with their rich pattern of accents, dialects, turns of phrase, intonations, speech rhythms and they are stored away in the mind. Often in Radio drama when doubling one or two minor parts with his leading role, Wilfred will ask how he should play a certain character—the Tax Inspector, perhaps. 'Like that chap we met at Moorside who'd won a lot of money, or a really cheerful type like Albert Wood the undertaker?' His same technique worked when it came to interviewing children. He'd never hurry them, never stand right over them, always treated them as individuals.

In the mid 1950s, as Organiser of Children's Programmes in the North, I wanted to see what sort of a fist we might offer with Television. After a Television Production course and a period working under that splendid innovator and

originator of many Children's Television Programmes,
Freda Lingstrom at Lime Grove, I felt bold enough to
approach Mabel about a television series with Wilfred. Not
unnaturally, she knew the man better than anyone else. In
the early days of working together on radio, I wondered why
Mabel always came with him, not necessarily for a studio
play or story reading, but certainly for the *Afternoon Out*
series. It soon became apparent that he worked all the better
when she was present; that those he would be interviewing
had someone else to talk to whilst they waited, someone
who was lively and appeared interested in them. And Mabel
was 'the listener' for Wilfred, for the scriptwriter and for
myself as producer, someone not so closely involved. She
asked some pretty searching questions about the ideas I had
for this new Sunday afternoon Magazine Programme.

'It'll be with and for young people?' asked Wilfred when
I'd satisfied his Front of House Manageress. Then he suggested
that a young person might share the introductions and the
interviews. Mary Malcolm and Macdonald Hobley were
the personalities who presented Children's Television programmes from London, but I was keen to try Geoffrey
Wheeler, Brian Trueman and Judith Chalmers who had
taken part in many plays and serials as teenagers and all
three had presented a Saturday afternoon Magazine Programme on Radio.

The man in charge of BBC Television Presentation was
then Rex Moorfoot. I hoped he might arrange for 16 year-old
Judith Chalmers to have an audition as a TV announcer but
she was at school during the weekdays and there were few
vision circuits available between London and Manchester at
weekends. So it was decided that her first appearance would
be her audition. The next wire from Rex stated 'She's fine',
so the forerunner of *Blue Peter* came onto the nation's screens
with Wilfred and Mabel Pickles assisted by Judith Chalmers
and a boat full of young people as we sailed up the river

Mersey for the opening programme. Putting the lettering, 'Children's Television Club' into large slabs of Blackpool rock became a sticky business as it happened to be a hot day for a later edition. A lot of pottery was 'thrown' by young hands and the National Soap Box Scout Derby was featured with Wilfred Pickles cutting quite a dashing figure until he suddenly seemed to slow and a six-year-old shouted, 'Hey, mister 'Y'wheels come off!'

Some of the best moments came out of interviews between young people who had made things—a sort of 'Inventor's Corner'. As he listened to the explanations of what things were *supposed* to do, never mind some of the *claims* that were made for certain products, Wilfred registered the complete gamut of facial emotion, from sheer incredulity—a quick look of 'Fancy that', perhaps, to a 'no, I mustn't laugh' expression. That was indicated by a sudden interest in his finger nail. But he will remember far more about those programmes. He'll remember even now the names of many youngsters who appeared with him in 'Children's Television Club'.

Not three summers since, he and Mabel joined Margaret and myself for a holiday on Lake Windermere. We boated a bit and visited various Lakeland places by car. One morning we'd been to Borrowdale and were heading for Cockermouth. Somewhere in or near Seatoller Wilfred said, 'If you turn up this lane, you'll come to a farm. I wonder if Noble and Amy Bland still live there!' He had been there once—twenty years ago. A woman was wheeling a pram across the yard as we pulled up. 'Hello', said Wilfred, 'Are your mother and father in?' They were. Perhaps such an accurate and retentive memory is something you are born with—or could it be the product of a mind that trained itself to memorise the part of Brutus in just two days?

Passing through Ambleside on the way back from visiting the Blands, Wilfred asked us to stop at Varty's bookshop. The son runs it now but many is the First Edition which Mr Varty—when he could be persuaded to part with any of his literary treasures, passed on to Wilfred. If the contents of a handbag tell you anything about a woman, then the contents of Wilfred Pickles' bookshelves tell you a lot about this particular man. The explanation for this lies many years back with the boy of fourteen whose appreciation and love of literature allowed him to spend the large sum of 5 shillings on a collection of Shakespeare.

Perhaps one of the most intimate acts lies between the reader and a book. It is an intensely personal business, as is the relationship between a reader and the listener, for as with the radio play it is a business of creating mental pictures. When television drama began to have an immense Sunday following in such splendid productions as *The Secret Garden*, one child wrote to say how much she enjoyed it but added, 'though I like the scenery best in radio plays'.

As a reader, besides a speaker of verse, Wilfred has had few equals. Having worked with Wilfred on many plays and serials, I wonder now what would be the reaction of his boyhood teacher of elocution. He would surely revel in the Pickles portrayal of 'the old ac-tor, laddie!' The voice which talks about 'the grr-and manor!' for this is surely Mr Ironmonger we are hearing. And Henry Baynton, for all the adulation he received from the young Pickles would surely feel, and with justification, that he must look to his acting laurels.

I was delighted to be able to call upon one of Wilfred's many voices in the very first drama production to come from the new Manchester Studio Centre in 1976, when William Keenan wrote *The Dark Windows of A Room* as a Saturday Night Theatre thriller.

Violet Carson, Billie Whitelaw, Bryan Forbes, Nigel Davenport, Philip Jenkinson, Geoffrey and Peter Wheeler, Alan Rothwell, Geoffrey Banks and Brian Trueman all came back to work again here with us in Manchester where they started their careers. Only Robert Powell was missing and as he got married the day he was required, he can be excused. Apart from Geoffrey and Brian, all those illustrious names did 'bit parts' as guest appearances. And Wilfred Pickles? Ah, he was the villain of the piece—a sleazy Viennese club owner, trafficking in human lives and drugs. I first heard that particular character from the walking repertory which is Wilfred Pickles when he did a long version of *Pilgrim's Progress* for the renowned D. G. Bridson. It was specially adapted for the occasion and re-titled *Wilfred Pilgrim's Progress*.

May he continue to do so.

ACKNOWLEDGEMENTS

After such a life in which I have had cause to be grateful to so many it would be iniquitous to single out a few names in the space available. I shall therefore confine myself to this book alone, so would like to express especial thanks to Lord Robens for providing the Foreword and to Trevor Hill for reviving so many happy memories with his Postscript.

I am grateful to Gerald Duckworth for permission to reprint the verse from Hilaire Belloc's *The South Country*, and to the Bodley Head for Arthur Benson's *My Will*.

My thanks, as always to Mabel, my wife, for her support and encouragement at all times and, last but certainly not least, to the people of these islands for their warmth, humour and good nature which has helped to make my own work so interesting and entertaining.

INDEX